SEASIDE
ARCHITECTURE

SEASIDE ARCHITECTURE

KENNETH LINDLEY

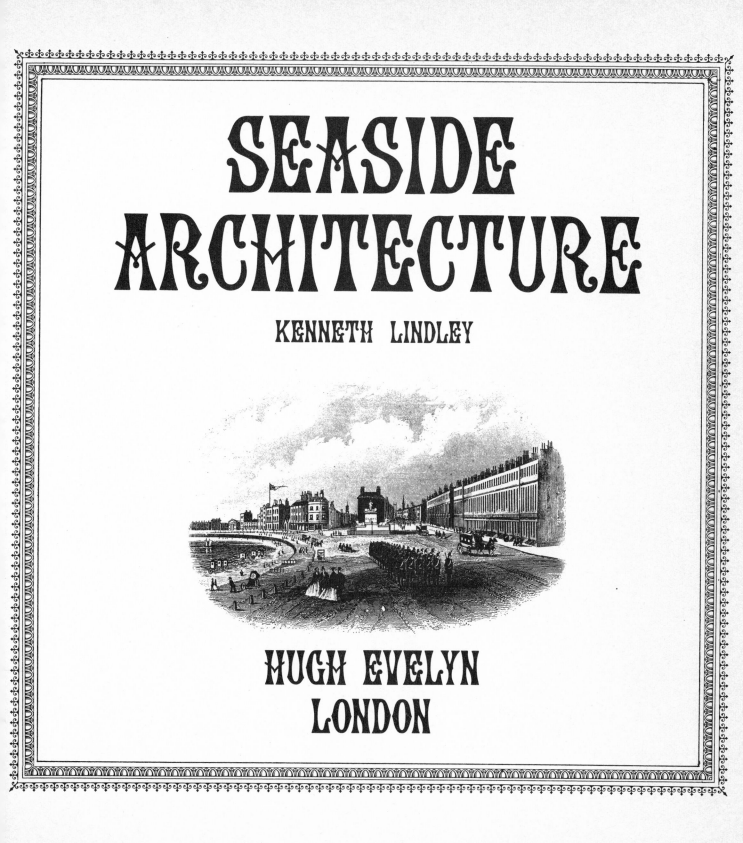

HUGH EVELYN
LONDON

To all who enjoy the seaside, whether they choose to do so from a
tent or a five star hotel; to my family, who come high on the list;
and to our many friends in the Caravan Club of Great Britain,
who by their responsible behaviour have proved that caravans
can make a valuable contribution to the use, improvement and
preservation of our coastline.

*'Her first idea was that she had somehow fallen into the sea, "and in
that case I can go back by railway," she said to herself. (Alice had
been to the seaside once in her life, and had come to the general
conclusion, that wherever you go to on the English coast you find a
number of bathing machines in the sea, some children digging in the
sand with wooden spades, then a row of lodging houses, and behind
them a railway station.)'*

Lewis Carroll, *Alice in Wonderland*, 1865

First published in 1973
by Hugh Evelyn Limited
9 Fitzroy Square, London W1P 5AH

©1973, Kenneth Lindley

SBN 238.78983.7

Designed by Norman-Reynolds

Printed in England
by Rockcliff Brothers Limited

Excursions into Architecture
SERIES EDITOR
David Braithwaite, A.A. Dipl., A.R.I.B.A.

CONTENTS

ACKNOWLEDGEMENTS

Many people have helped in various ways in the preparation of this book and I am gratefully aware of the contributions they have made. In particular I must thank Mr F. Bolland for very extensive information on the history of slot machines, and Mr Holloway of the Samson Novelty Company for further help on the same subject.

The managers and proprietors of numerous hotels, piers and other establishments have answered my enquiries with patience and thoroughness, as have the officers of many seaside resorts. Various trade and professional organisations have responded in a similarly helpful way and I would like to add a final and special note of gratitude to fellow members of the Railway and Canal Historical Society for the willingness with which the results of personal researches have been shared.

INTRODUCTION

Weymouth from the north. A charming mid-nineteenth century view which conveys the flavour of the period

The association between the seaside and the concept of holidays and pleasure is entirely English and of comparatively recent origin. After all, until well into the last century the population was divided into two main groups; those who had no holidays and those whose income placed them above the necessity of regular employment. In such a situation holidays as we know them could hardly exist. Significantly, the only times when workmen were temporarily freed from the oppression of continuous employment were Sundays and holy days which, in a predominantly Puritan country such as Victorian England, were few and far between. It was not until well into the present century that an Englishman could regard Sunday as a day for anything other than religious observance without inviting the disapproval of a conventional society which usually included among its more prominent members his own employers. The growth of the seaside as a holiday place and pleasure ground has therefore been closely linked to developments in, among others, social and religious attitudes, economic change, transport and mobility, education, and the upward surge first of the middle and later of the working classes.

Until the eighteenth century the sea and the coastline were regarded as the province of the sailor and fisherman, and best avoided. Those who faced the perils of the sea were a strange and hardy breed, eulogised in romantic literature but not to be encountered at close quarters. Even in the latter part of the nineteenth century the authors of a much used series of guides were advising tourists always to make sure they outnumbered the boatmen when taking pleasure trips along the Yorkshire coast, because of the rough and untrustworthy natures of those characters. Even in the mid-twentieth century, for all our sophistication, the sea is still a force to be reckoned with as well as enjoyed, for it can claim a luxury liner or supertanker as effectively as it can a Whitby coble. The demands it makes upon people and the inanimate objects with which it comes into contact are equally severe whatever the purpose of the encounter.

DEAL by J.M.W. Turner (1775-1851). The ferocity of sea and storm (note the wrecks), buildings with their backs to the sea and fishermen struggling with their boats hardly indicate that the seaside is the ideal place for holidays. Turner's working life spanned the period during which the coast was transformed from working ports and fishing villages to a landscape for holidays and pleasure and both extremes provided subject matter for his romantic imagery

For centuries men have been driven by necessity or the urge for adventure to meet the sea on its own terms, and in order to do so have required not only ports and harbours but also all the fascinating impedimenta of nautical activity. Quays, lighthouses, slipways, seawalls and all the other ingredients typical of the seaside landscape have evolved their characteristic forms over long years of trial and error and bitter experience of the power of the sea. So demanding is the sea that the shape and construction of such works have been reduced to a kind of ultra-functional state as dateless as it is unique to its particular situation. History may inform us that this harbour was planned and built by the Romans and that by Telford, but to the casual observer the differences are slight. The disciplines imposed upon the design of seaside structures become even more apparent when they are compared with other buildings of their own period.

Faced with such stringent demands and considering the fear and horror with which the sea was almost universally regarded it is hardly surprising that its association with pleasure is a phenomenon of recent history. Such an association is essentially a landsman's attitude. Even now it is possible to find towns on the north-east coast of England and elsewhere which turn their backs to the sea. In Northumberland and on parts of the Yorkshire coast rows of fishermen's cottages along the sea's edge back on to the seawall, preferring to turn their faces inland. It is in places such as these that the desolation of the sea can be felt even more strongly than where the house-high Atlantic waves break against the rocks of Cornwall.

The pleasure buildings of the seaside with which this book is concerned are a world apart from those cottages or the great harbour walls of an exposed coastline. Yet they share the same need to withstand the forces of nature and have a character that is unmistakably coastal. Many, probably most, of the buildings associated with seaside holidays and pleasure resorts have their inland equivalents but they are never quite the same. A combina-

Below
BRIGHTHELMSTON (Brighton) by J.M.W. Turner. The transitional stage between fishing village and resort. Fishermen still battle against the unyielding water and the town appears to be suspended between equally hostile sky and sea, but the Pavilion dominates the centre of the picture and promenaders on the Chain Pier can share the fishermen's experience of the waves without the attendant dangers

Right
Sidmouth. Regency villa forming part of a terrace facing the sea. The scale here is domestic in contrast to the grandiose compositions at Brighton and is indicative of the origins of seaside architecture for genteel families. This delightful building, with its fashionable 'gothick' detail and coloured glass windows is representative of the change from vernacular cottage to fashionable residence which transformed so much of the English coast at the beginning of the nineteenth century

Below
ILFRACOMB by J.M.W. Turner. An illustration of the wildly romantic attitude to the coast which dominated seaside development for nearly a century. The town shelters behind its protective headland. Walkers on the cliffs are participants in the great drama of sea and sky played out against an incomparable landscape setting. The wreck, with men clinging to the rigging, provides the essential tragic element

Bottom
Brighton Pavilion, designed by John Nash and built between 1815 and 1823. Nash, who started his career as a speculative builder, was a true man of his age. He possessed immaculate taste and an eye for landscape which enabled him to design buildings in landscape with a success seldom surpassed. His greatest work was the modelling of London from Buckingham Palace to Regents Park. The Brighton Pavilion has frequently been regarded as an aberration and has narrowly escaped destruction, but it is now recognised as a work of genius. Whatever fashionable opinion may be of its merits, its effect on seaside architecture cannot be exaggerated

tion of salt air and an indefinable seaside spirit make them delightfully though often inexplicably different.

The rise of the seaside resort in the Regency period, with its flowering in the reign of Victoria, was a happy coincidence. There was then an adventurous approach to life, and excitement over new ideas and new materials produced almost perfect conditions for the evolution of seaside architecture and all its decorative accompaniments. The eighteenth century was the age of the spa, the nineteenth the age of the resort. Among seaside spas in England two were pre-eminent, Brighton in the south and Scarborough facing the North Sea in Yorkshire. Surprisingly, the medicinal properties of the mineral spring at Scarborough were discovered as early as 1620 but it was not until 1698 that a serious attempt was made to develop its potential by the construction of cisterns to store the water. The first Spa House was built in 1700. Its construction signalled a change of attitude which was to transform the coastlines of practically every civilised country over the next century and a half. The process is still going on.

For probably the first time people were turning to the sea for their health and thus, very shortly, for their pleasure. Those who were in a position to take health cures came from a social class whose major interest in life was pleasure. The cure itself can hardly have been a pleasurable activity for it was considered that for maximum effect one had to suffer the maximum of discomfort. When sea bathing was included (as it soon was, along with the drinking of sea water) it had to be undertaken in the winter when the temperature was at its lowest. Whether or not the popular expression 'to kill or cure' had its origins in this practice is not known but it must certainly have been appropriate.

Compared with Scarborough, Brighton was a late starter. In the middle of the eighteenth century it was still only a small collection of fishermen's huts, 'scarcely known, even by name' as an early nineteenth century gazetteer recalls. From 1750 until it became a centre of wealth and fashion under the patronage of

George IV the rise of Brighton was rapid and spectacular. Its
famous Pavilion, designed by John Nash as a fantasia of caricatured
oriental styles of architecture, was begun in 1784. It can justifiably
be regarded as a prototype of seaside architecture for the next 100
years and its onion domes and vaguely oriental decoration were
echoed in piers and pavilions from Blackpool to Margate. Although
it was a seaside building almost by accident its display of frivolous
forms and decoration opened the eyes of subsequent designers to
the possibilities of the fantastic in architecture as a setting for
enjoyment. Its royal owner gave the necessary seal of approval.
The Pavilion transformed the country gentleman's private conceit
of the 'folly' into an acceptable form of public building. It was also
a landmark in the change from the architecture of good taste to
that of ostentation. The latter, so essentially part of Victorian
England, was ideally suited to exploitation by the developers of
seaside resorts.

The eighteenth century spa was the playground of the idle
and the rich, its architecture reflecting the taste and fashion of the
day. In general terms the nineteenth century resort met the needs
of slightly lower grades of society and it reflected their tastes and
standards. The eighteenth century gentleman, with his town and
country houses and his own accommodation in one of the spa
terraces, needed no hotels unless he was actually travelling. Then
he had to make use of inns which were usually well below his own
standards. But the nineteenth century merchant or professional
man who took his family on an annual holiday to the seaside
needed an hotel, and he expected it to be a little grander than his
own home. He was paying in hard-earned cash for his pleasures,
and a show of high or even ostentatious living was part of what he
expected. The rise of the prosperous middle class dates from the
industrial revolution and the boost it gave to the merchant,
entrepreneur and self-made man. The first seaside hotels catered
for the carriage trade of these newly rich. Almost at the same time
came the railway boom, changing both the landscape and the

Bangor pier. The longterm influence of the Brighton Pavilion. The detail may be coarser but the basic forms, and the atmosphere, are nearly identical. The heavy cast-iron gates and even the painted boards are consistent in their use of exaggerated forms (eg, of acanthus and Roman letters) for decorative effect. The modern sans-serif letters of 'Pier Toll' and the stark tubular rail on the right of the picture show how unsympathetic functionalism is to the seaside holiday spirit

Brighton Pavilion as seen by Cruikshank. The accompanying verse begins:

– The queerest of all the queer sights
 I've set sight on:–
Is, the what d'ye-call-t thing, here,
 The Folly at Brighton
The outside – huge teapots,
 all drill'd round with holes,
Relieved by extinguishers,
 sticking on poles:
The inside – all tea-things,
 and dragons, and bells,
The show rooms – all show,
 the sleeping rooms – cells.

social habits of the nation within a decade.

The railways turned dozens of obscure, even hitherto non-existent, seaside villages into holiday resorts within an incredibly short time. Much of the development was undertaken by companies set up for this purpose, sometimes by the railways themselves. It was an age of supreme optimism and it showed in the amount and in the character of much of the building that was undertaken. The triumphant passage of the Great Western Railway and its subsidiaries opened up the south and west. Development of Torquay began in 1820, that at Teignmouth a decade or so earlier. The esplanade at Sidmouth was constructed in 1837; the 'Cornish Riviera' was beginning to appear. Similar things were happening wherever the railways reached the coast, and many seaside towns can be accurately dated from the architecture of their major buildings and their railway station. The process continued throughout the century and beyond (Cromer and Sheringham are predominantly Edwardian). The railways did more than make possible a totally new kind of coastal town. They offered the prospect of travel to whole sections of the population who had hitherto never known anything of the world beyond walking distance from their own birthplaces. They introduced the day trip and even the weekend to a new generation of artisans and mechanics bent on enjoying what little leisure they were able to earn.

Bank Holidays were not introduced in England until 1871, but by then the coast was well prepared to receive the impact of thousands of city dwellers on the loose for a day. Many of the characteristic features of trips to the seaside date from that period. Once again many seaside towns were changing their role and appearance. Genteel middle class families retreated (as they still do) from those towns, or parts of them, frequented by day trippers, from their rash of amusements, funfairs, slot machines and attendant vulgarities. It was, however, in the years between the two wars that the English resort really came into its own and

Lynmouth. Stages in seaside development. On the left, cottages in the vernacular tradition. In the centre, a typical early nineteenth century seaside villa with later additions. Above, the monstrously out of scale Torrs Hotel, mock half-timbered and aggressively painted in cream and green

boarding houses first outnumbered hotels. Edwardian terra-cotta and redbrick piles, which had themselves displaced Victorian cast-iron structures as the most popular of seaside forms of building, gave way to new concoctions of chrome and coloured glass, like the 'Blue Lagoon' at Clacton-on-Sea. The wealthier classes, who had discovered the Italian and French Rivieras at the turn of the century and had thus transformed the Mediterranean coast from Chiavari to Nice, were looking farther afield.

Since the Second World War another transformation has taken place. The aeroplane is doing on a European scale what the railways did on a national scale over a century ago, and many families now fly from England to the Mediterranean for their annual holidays. In doing so they have not only stimulated the growth of Mediterranean coastal building to almost gold rush proportions but have also precipitated fairly drastic changes back at home. Where an earlier generation had demanded almost regal splendours when holidaying on the English coast the new generation demands the very latest in architectural and electronic developments and fashions at its newly discovered sunspots. An eruption of vast concrete hotels and new resorts in which every known architectural device is exploited in the interests of novelty is spreading along the coasts of southern Europe and northern Africa like an epidemic. It is no new phenomenon in the United States, where Hollywood can be traced as the source of many of the wilder architectural excesses which in turn sprang from the glamourised view of highlife propagated by its films.

From a world whose inhabitants mostly kept to themselves and their homes we have changed within little more than a century and a half to a world of seething populations who chase restlessly farther and farther afield for their pleasures. Mobility is now the keynote and with it goes a constant demand for novelty. Not only do seaside buildings change to meet this demand (and disposable plastic façades are already with us) but completely new approaches to holidays have become possible. Every year hundreds of

17

thousands of cars and caravans swarm across the English Channel
in both directions, creating a demand for campsites and their
attendant facilities. These have the tremendous advantage of being
temporary; out of season the tents and caravans disappear, leaving
landscapes virtually untouched and enjoying a necessary interval
of rest between the periods of frenzied activity of the summer
months. Temporary or otherwise, the campsite is now as essential
to the holiday scene as the hotel or boarding house. So is the
holiday camp and the static caravan site. All have their peculiar
forms and requirements, and each creates an environment
peculiarly its own. They represent some of the few entirely special
forms of seaside architecture, like Victorian piers or inter-war
pavilions.

Much of what we associate with the seaside is temporary and
ephemeral, and this adds to its attraction. Confronted by an
inland sea of caravans and chalets echoing the real sea across a
narrow strip of sand or shingle, one may reflect that, unlike the
vast Victorian Grand Hotels, they can be changed or cleared
within a very short time. They are not likely to present problems
to future generations whose ideas about holidays and landscapes
may differ from ours. Perhaps it is part of the holiday fun that we
know it cannot last. We should welcome the technological progress
that makes it possible to throw away a building (a chalet or
caravan) almost as easily as a postcard or fancy hat.

Old slot machines are now collectors' pieces and there are
few objects closer to the pulse of popular demand than amusement
machines. The larger than life cast-iron chickens which would
lay a present in a cardboard egg for a couple of pennies are, in
their way, like the Grand Hotels with their mixture of pomposity
and frivolity. They are symbols of the seaside and its architecture,
to be wondered at, enjoyed and then forgotten, but never to be
taken too seriously.

Chapter 1

ALONG THE PROMENADE

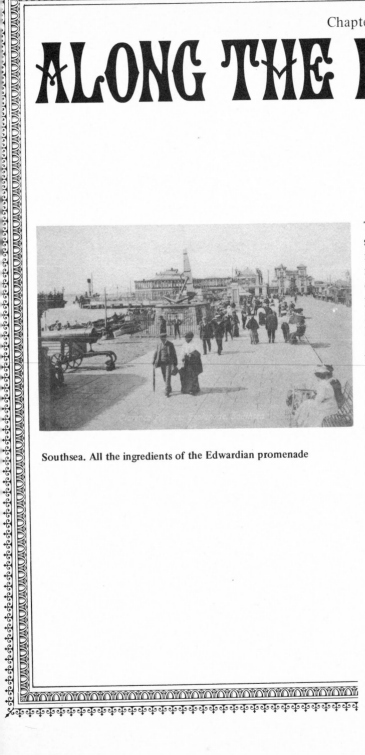

Southsea. All the ingredients of the Edwardian promenade

The indefinable character we think of at the mention of the word seaside is nowhere more apparent than along that strip of no man's land between beach and buildings, the promenade. The name conjures up memories of walks along breezy cliff tops; of evening concerts by brass bands, the fairy lights reflected in polished buttons and instruments; of bank holiday picnics on the greensward (although not, of course, at Frinton where such plebeian delights are forbidden); of obstacle golf and paddling pools; of faded postcards showing thin men in bowlers and women in long skirts; of basketwork bath chairs. The construction of the promenade was the first step in the transformation of a stretch of coastline into a resort, for it asserted man's mastery of the elements and stabilised the immediate shoreline against the encroachments of the sea. It was evidence of the change from working vernacular to holiday landscape. It provided a place where holidaymakers could walk after dinner, breathing the ozone, displaying their holiday clothes, and passing the time in pleasant conversation in the way many Italian families still parade with their children in the piazzas on summer evenings. Old postcards often reveal throngs of long-skirted women and men in dark suits taking the air 'along the prom'. The habit has all but gone, but the name and its associations remain.

It was the promenade which gave a town its particular character. Along it you would find that strange collection of objects ranging from cast-iron shelters to flagmasts which together made up the seaside image. Here, the massive functionalism of seawalls combined with the frivolities of rustic fencing or fancy ironwork. Much of the detail is ephemeral in character, even if it has lasted a century, and it has an appropriate jollity. It is mainly composed of that strange mixture of nautical functionalism and the joyfully unrestrained which is the key to the charm of urban seaside landscape. It is seen at its best in those resorts which achieved the climax of their development at the turn of the century and which have managed to resist the tendency to become

Budleigh Salterton. Beach objects

seaside suburbs. The effect of its absence can best be appreciated in those dreary estates of suburban bungalows and semi-detacheds which have been spreading like a plague along those areas of English coastline made accessible as commuter country by the Southern Railway and its successor. Such areas as the Sussex coast east of Brighton provide ample proof that the chance juxtaposition of buildings and coast does not necessarily produce seaside architecture. A sensitivity for *locale* is sadly lacking in most speculative builders.

The promenade produced, ancillary to its main function, a wealth of minor architectural forms and details. It provided a natural collecting ground for all kinds of objects which may be found individually elsewhere but which (and this is important) only came together in this way at the seaside. The Edwardian seaside promenade is a contribution to landscape design as significant in its way as the Regency crescent, and all the more interesting for its apparently casual origins. It must have seemed natural enough, once the promenade or esplanade was built, to embellish it with monuments, gardens and decorative ironwork, and to provide such facilities as seats, shelters or public lavatories. From such small beginnings some exciting landscapes grew.

Where the land met the sea without the interruption of a cliff, as at Southsea, the paved promenade formed a link between the road and buildings on one side and the sea and beach on the other: it became a fascinating dividing line between wild nature and ordered civilisation. It was built, wisely, on a level with the shingle and without any dividing wall or rail. Platforms projected on to the beach to support shelters of a beautifully delicate design and an assortment of nautical monuments. The resultant view from the Esplanade towards Clarence Pier could only be in England, and at the seaside. Much of the original detail remains, but old photographs reveal the unrepeatable period flavour. Seats delicately wrought from a lattice of iron rods and slats support women in long dresses and large hats, often sheltering from the sun beneath large black umbrellas. Among the crowd are the ubiquitous sailors and a few obvious locals, but they are outnumbered by holidaymakers. A departing paddle steamer is framed between the ironwork of a shelter and the distant pavilion of Clarence Pier. On one side of the promenaders are the boats drawn up on to the beach, and the succession of monuments which characterise Southsea; on the other is a street trader with his barrow, and a line of open horse carriages awaiting hire. Every detail appears to be perfectly related to the whole and nothing is out of place.

The proximity of Portsmouth with its long standing naval traditions had an obvious influence on Southsea. Elsewhere other influences had their effect. Along the flat Suffolk coast the town of Aldeburgh, developed in Victorian times by Newson Garrett, gains its character from the fishermen's paraphernalia on the beach. Here as at Southsea the paved promenade gives directly on to the shingle, but Aldeburgh, like other resorts that were no more than enlarged fishing villages, was remote from the larger centres of population and, served only by a branch line, acquired no sophisticated monuments, piers or pavilions. The fishing boats, blue and white against the grey-brown shingle, are tenuously attached to winches by thin lines of rusted cable: piles of fish boxes or lobster baskets, and triangular signs marking the end of a seaward obstruction, these are the features which can have changed little since the Victorians developed a taste for the bracing east coast. The difference between the seafronts at Aldeburgh and Southsea is essentially the difference between the Victorian holiday, when pebble collecting was an obsession and shell boxes and shell pictures in heart-shaped frames served as year-long reminders between vacations, and the sophistication of the Edwardian era and the twentieth century pleasures of the funfair, the concert parties, illuminations and candyfloss. The attraction of the promenade lies in the fact that the unsophisticated always seems about to impinge.

Right
Folkestone. The Leas bandstand. A good example of an essential component of any seaside resort from the end of the nineteenth until the mid-twentieth century. The encrustation with light bulbs is a major twentieth century contribution to the holiday atmosphere

Below
Folkestone. 'The Leas at Folkestone are indisputably one of the finest marine promenades in the world. It consists of a spacious carriage-drive with promenades and walks situated on the top of the cliffs commanding magnificent views of the shore and Channel. There are shelters and an excellent bandstand for the accommodation and entertainment of visitors'

Morecambe. A coin in the slot telescope with strange mammalian qualities

Where a cliff or spectacular change of level occurred between town and beach the promenade could take advantage of the situation and extend its influence to cliff walks and a split level existence. The urbanity of Brighton and the scale of its upper and lower levels is unmatched by any other English resort, although its influence can be traced along the French Riviera and elsewhere on the continent. The redbrick and terra-cotta landscape of Biarritz's front and the tiered promenade of San Sebastian are examples of the Edwardian influence. More typical of the English seaside is an odd mixture of quaint rustic (which usually lapses into banality in any other situation), the whimsical and functional, all touched by the romantic tradition of landscape design. The Leas at Folkestone provide an excellent example. The top level is a generous expanse of greensward between the hotels and the cliff, on which stands a superb bandstand surrounded at the appropriate season by its attendent mass of deckchairs. The bandstand, like an enormous birdcage, is typical of this strange but now familiar architectural form at the height of its development. The canopy, displaying just the right amount of ornament derived from sources as diverse as China and classical antiquity, is dominated by a kind of cupola topped by a weather vane. The whole is supported by eight slender iron columns branching at the top into openwork brackets which appear in silhouette as pierced capitals. Between these columns glass screens slide on runners to protect the bandsmen from the wind. An ornate rail connects the base of the columns and the whole structure stands on a low plinth. The wind screens are a later addition as are the loudspeakers (themselves rapidly becoming period pieces in design) and the myriad coloured light bulbs with which the whole thing is encrusted.

The change of level from the Leas to the lower road and beach is used to great effect, the cliff being well covered by trees and shrubs and traversed by numerous paths cunningly devised to make the most of the existing formation. The zigzag path shows how well this has been done, using the textbook forms of romantic

Harwich. The Angel public house. A Victorian building which admirably illustrates the local vernacular with a few period details. This group of buildings contrasts with the mock grandeur of the adjacent Town Hall (Great Eastern Hotel) and the architecturally nondescript ferry terminal across the road. As shown in the illustration it is the virtually unaltered landscape of a 'comfortable' rather than prosperous working port of the early nineteenth century

landscape: rocks, tunnels, overhanging foliage and a mass of introduced, but apparently indigenous, plants. The scale of the landscape at Folkestone makes ornamental gardens as such unnecessary. The shelters built into the cliff at various levels provide adequate protection and seating, with splendid views and without the need to encroach on the open expanse of the Leas.

Other resorts that lack such natural advantages solved the problem by constructing a series of ornamental gardens between buildings and beach or, alternatively, made a clear distinction between an essentially urban promenade and separate parks and gardens. The seafront at Scarborough for example has managed to retain the character of a working port at one end of its South Bay and a spa at the other, both of which blend into a delightful but essentially urban landscape. Peasholm Park, with its boating lake on which mock sea battles are fought in miniature boats, its passenger-carrying model railway and open air theatre, is at the extreme end of North Bay and there are other gardens at the southern end of the town. Here, as at Folkestone, a cliff of magnificent proportions provides a natural feature which has been fully exploited. Where no such readymade landscape features exist, artifice has to supply the need.

The low cliff at Clacton-on-Sea is sufficient to provide the view necessary to a good promenade but is not a very interesting feature in its own right. The sloping paths, low shrubs and rustic fencing which have been worked on to it seem to be perfectly in scale with the place and help to give Clacton its unusual quality of compromise between seaside and a more domestic landscape. In atmosphere as well as situation Clacton stands between the claustrophobic domesticity of Frinton and the brash, exuberant urbanity of Southend. The string of neat gardens stretching along the front from the pier to the point where the town peters out in a mess of funfairs, holiday camps and chalets is as important a part of the whole holiday landscape as the pier itself. The concrete bridge carrying the promenade over the road leading down to the

pier has exactly the same character as the gardens and the rustic fencing. In spite of its increasing day trip trade and attractions the promenade at Clacton preserves the air of quiet gentility which has been a characteristic of the place for generations. The raucous funfairs are at one end of the promenade, and the crowds are channelled along Pier Avenue and on to the beach leaving the upper promenade level, with its gardens, ponds and putting greens, its seats and shelters, for the elderly and its greensward for family picnics.

Where the expanse of land available between town and sea is greater the opportunities increase. At Skegness a boating canal runs through a continuous strip of ornamental gardens which seem to set off the wide beaches left by the receding tide. At Lytham St Annes the gardens contain an interesting collection of shelters, monuments and other attractions, marred by the wholly inappropriate redbrick entrance to the pier. Many of the iron objects were cast in the Sun Foundry, Glasgow, and a stroll along the front is like walking through the pages of a late nineteenth century ironfounder's catalogue. Chinese style shelters topped by dragons seem perfectly at home on the Lancashire coast in such unlikely company as cast-iron fountains and a stone memorial to the lifeboat crew. This latter object befits its setting and gives it point, in the way a monument to a mine disaster can focus heroism and misery through a single symbol which seems to link men and landscape in a particularly significant way. The lifeboatman on his monument at St Annes epitomises that mixture of danger and excitement which the sea engenders and through which it leaves its mark on both buildings and people. It is not great sculpture but it is certainly good landscape.

This is, perhaps, another key to understanding the seaside. In any landscape the individual components are less important than overall character. A sense of locality is much more necessary than the ability to produce otherwise commendable architecture which might lack an essential relationship, visually or in the less

FRESH
JELLIED
EELS

SCARBOROUGH
OAK SMOKED
KIPPERS
46
AND EELS

SCARBOROUGH
OAK·SMOKED
KIPPERS

Whelks, Cockles, Mussels   OYSTERS 3

KIPPERS POSTED

Local Caught **CRABS**
& LOBSTERS

ORDERS TAKEN

TROUT

Our Own
CATCH

B. BAYES.

Fresh
OYSTERS. COCKLES.
WHELKS, MUSSELS
& Winkles

fresh JELLIE
EEL

KIPPERS
FRESH

S.

CRAB

Boiled
FRESH
DAILY

Scarborough. The display is the building, the structure being merely a framework for placards and produce and a background animated by stall-holders and their customers

tangible terms of the spirit of the place, with its neighbours. In this context the shellfish stalls, the arrays of plastic buckets and beach balls, the rock and the candyfloss are often more significant than the ten storey dream of a respected architect. A particularly interesting example of such sensitivity towards place is a jellied eel bar by the road leading to the older part of the seafront at Hastings. The fascination of this part of Hastings lies in its collection of oddly proportioned net sheds. These are of wood, horizontally boarded and preserved beneath layers of pitch. They are all several times higher than they are broad and the effect of groups of them on the multi-coloured shingle is unique. The jellied eel bar echoes their shapes without copying them and thus is perfectly in keeping. At the same time it provides a link between the quaint end of Hastings and the newer resort to the west. Its success is enhanced by its traditional signwriting and the two signwriter's paintings of appropriate scenes which decorate the façade. This must all have been a conscious (but delightfully unpretentious) exercise in design. Elsewhere similar effects are achieved with the lack of conscious awareness that is the hallmark of vernacular art.

The row of stalls alongside the fish quay at Scarborough illustrate the point. The actual construction of corrugated iron and girders is so undistinguished as to go unnoticed. The real construction, at least visually, is in the signboards, the displays on the canted slabs and the people who serve and are served. The stallholders stand on platforms like actors on a stage, giving movement on two levels. The lettering on placards or upturned fishboxes, the varieties of whelks, cockles, mussels, crabs, eels, oysters and kippers, displayed in piles or neat rows or inside glass jars: these are the components of a varied and constantly changing scene. Similar effects are to be seen at almost any English seaside, whether the stalls are offering local kippers, rock or tickets for a trip round the bay.

In summer the promenades are animated by bustling crowds

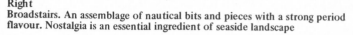

of holidaymakers and the bright colours of stalls and beach equipment. Out of season those expanses of grass and paving which were so necessary a background to the summer bustle become bleak areas of rain-swept desert across which residents battle their way to the shelters. It is easy to forget that many resorts began their existence as year-round places and attempts to establish a prolonged season are in many cases a move towards original intentions. The cast-iron shelters with their glazed wind shields were meant to keep out the storms of the winter as much as the sun of summer. The promenades too were intended for winter as well as for summer use, and even the most apparently insubstantial of seaside constructions has to be built either to withstand the gales or be dismantled at the end of each season.

The collecting boxes made from First World War mines stand through the winter, as do some of the coin-operated telescopes and other characteristic objects. These telescopes perch like nocturnal creatures on their poles, proof that even things as delicate as optical instruments and timing mechanisms can be conditioned by their situation so that by function rather than conscious design they resemble the instruments of a ship's bridge.

Below the promenades or between the greens and gardens· and the sea, at the point where the waves meet the first line of the land, there is no room for compromise. The seawall itself has but one function, to protect the land against the encroachments of the seas. For at least a century this meeting point has aroused an inquisitive wonder. Early prints and souvenir albums show pictures of mighty seas crashing against the sea defences, and later postcards repeated the pattern. To send to absent friends a view of the esplanade in front of your hotel with waves breaking across it two storeys high was to suggest that you were experiencing something of the terrors of the ocean. What is more to the point is that the architectural forms and methods of construction required to withstand such a battering allow for no compromise. The pure functionalism of seawalls is one of the least recognised delights in

Harwich. The emergence of the new landscape of the weekend yachtsman. The development of plastics has added significantly to the effect of colour on coastal landscape

Below
Worthing. A bulb-encrusted lamp standard which debunks the pomposity of much municipal design and becomes a vigorous sculptural object by day or night

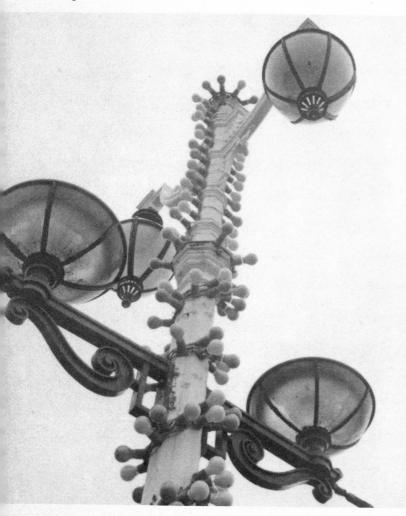

Margate. A well-designed public lavatory which fits neatly into a visual jumble of boats, pier pavilions and other details. The excellent lettering is in the best monumental traditions and indicates that the genteel Roman and sans-serif alphabets which were so universally applied to public buildings between the wars are now forgotten

Below
Brightlingsea. Between-wars hotel and post-war yacht club. Two sophisticated buildings with a small vernacular shed between illustrating recent changes in attitude. The hotel dominates, the club belongs

the history of architecture. Lighthouses, harbour walls and dock installations have been chronicled and admired, but the seawall has yet to be discovered.

Along the eastern coast of England there is a constant battle against erosion. All of the Holderness coast for some 30 or more miles between Bridlington and Spurn Head is crumbling into the sea at a rate of several feet a year. Along the beaches of Yorkshire, Lincolnshire and East Anglia the evidence of attempts to stop erosion make up a collection of sculptural shapes, themselves as characteristic of the seaside as driftwood or a harbour bollard. Wooden breakwaters, stone groynes, metal markers or twisted piling are the first line of defence and they take the hardest battering. They break the impact of the water against the walls of the promenades and are broken in the process. The walls themselves must be firmer and more massively constructed. Along the flat coastline of Lincolnshire the walls have to perform their task unaided by nature, and the resultant massive constructions of flat and inclined planes, with curves to throw the water back upon itself, have a strength and beauty that were first revealed in the paintings of Paul Nash. Even such an undistinguished place as Sutton-on-Sea has a scale and a magnificence about its seawall and breakwaters that is entirely lacking in the hinterland they protect. Where the land is even more low-lying then the sea defences become correspondingly more impressive. At Dymchurch, where Nash made the drawings for his paintings of the sea and its walls, the scale of the masonry is beautifully contrasted to the forest of wooden posts of the breakwaters. The sweep of the wall which protects the marshland between Frinton and Clacton in Essex is another example of the dominance of functional form where it is essential. This wall carries a seafront footpath from the bungalows of Holland-on-Sea to the wide greensward of Frinton and is in total contrast to the cosiness of both. Beneath the spa buildings and later municipal rockeries of Scarborough is a vaultlike under-structure as stark as an Egyptian tomb and mysterious as a Piranesi

catacomb. Such juxtapositions are the essence of seaside landscape and architecture.

So also are the relationships between those buildings which remain in the vernacular idiom and those with a more self-conscious appearance. When fishing villages first began their metamorphosis into fashionable resorts their architectural additions deliberately avoided the commonplace of, for instance, existing cottages. They displayed an awareness of high fashion with sophisticated pride. Even so the vernacular not only continued to exist but flourished alongside many of the more fashionable areas. Many resorts led a double life as holiday towns and working ports and harbours, and many generations of holidaymakers have relished the situation. Visitors would descend from their hotels on the clifftop at Whitby to watch the cobles fighting their way into the harbourmouth, and the fishmarket has always been a source of interest to visitors. Wherever the two functions remain, as they do at many resorts, the contrast between work and pleasure as expressed architecturally produces a unique landscape form. In many instances it is as extreme as if a coalmine had been established in Regency Bath, with the comings and goings of the miners proclaimed as a major attraction.

Such a contrast can be seen between the east and west ends of Folkestone or between the old town and the modern resort at San Sebastian. Even this is likely to be lost as yachtsmen begin to outnumber fishermen and old cottages are converted into weekend bungalows. While it remains, this juxtaposition of vernacular and sophisticated building is a significant part of seaside landscape. Although the earliest buildings of the new resorts fastidiously avoided the features of pre-existing local architecture, over the years the charm of the vernacular has been recognised and, occasionally, consciously adapted.

The English coast is rich in buildings which display local solutions to local problems using local materials. Essex is still fortunate in having sufficient weather-boarded buildings to give

San Sebastian. The nautical image for seaside fun

distinction to whole areas of small towns such as Harwich or
Brightlingsea. A particularly interesting illustration of the way in
which attitudes have changed during the course of a century can
be seen in examples from these two places. The white-painted,
weather-boarded Angel public house at Harwich is one of a group
of buildings which are excellent examples of building methods
peculiar to the locality. The nearby town hall (once the Great
Eastern Hotel) is in extreme and deliberate contrast. At
Brightlingsea the recently built customs house is a simple and
pleasant modern building which sympathetically responds to
the older boatsheds which are its immediate neighbours, and
is thus a continuation of a local form and tradition. Such
buildings as the Brightlingsea customs house or the boat-shaped
pavilion at San Sebastian are evidence of the completion of a cycle
which has taken more than a century and a half to achieve.

The earliest resorts were models (later to become caricatures)
of high fashion, consciously scorning the rustic crudities of their
antecedents. Gradually the fishermen and other coast dwellers and
men of the sea became part of the romantic holiday notion. They
were admired from the safety of pier and promenade, or even
joined when the weather was suitable on fishing expeditions and
trips round the bay. Even so, for a century or more the landscape
and architecture of holiday resorts and working ports were kept
distinct (though not always apart). It is in comparatively recent
times that the two have begun to merge. The terrors of the sea
have to some extent been subjugated by technology, which has
made sailing and navigation the sport of millions of amateurs.
Mass holidays and the breakdown of many formalities of
behaviour have also brought the sophisticated and the vernacular
close to the point of merging, and such distinctions as remain are
increasingly blurred. The resulting landscapes have a freshness
and vitality which are already beginning to extend the concept of
the seaside in new directions.

Chapter 2

PIERS AND PAVILIONS

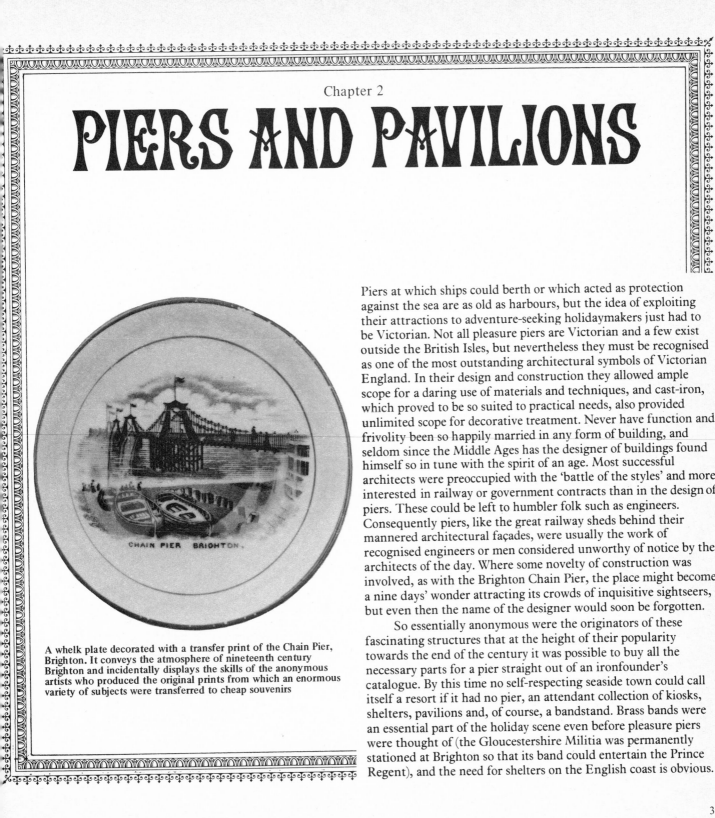

A whelk plate decorated with a transfer print of the Chain Pier, Brighton. It conveys the atmosphere of nineteenth century Brighton and incidentally displays the skills of the anonymous artists who produced the original prints from which an enormous variety of subjects were transferred to cheap souvenirs

Piers at which ships could berth or which acted as protection against the sea are as old as harbours, but the idea of exploiting their attractions to adventure-seeking holidaymakers just had to be Victorian. Not all pleasure piers are Victorian and a few exist outside the British Isles, but nevertheless they must be recognised as one of the most outstanding architectural symbols of Victorian England. In their design and construction they allowed ample scope for a daring use of materials and techniques, and cast-iron, which proved to be so suited to practical needs, also provided unlimited scope for decorative treatment. Never have function and frivolity been so happily married in any form of building, and seldom since the Middle Ages has the designer of buildings found himself so in tune with the spirit of an age. Most successful architects were preoccupied with the 'battle of the styles' and more interested in railway or government contracts than in the design of piers. These could be left to humbler folk such as engineers. Consequently piers, like the great railway sheds behind their mannered architectural façades, were usually the work of recognised engineers or men considered unworthy of notice by the architects of the day. Where some novelty of construction was involved, as with the Brighton Chain Pier, the place might become a nine days' wonder attracting its crowds of inquisitive sightseers, but even then the name of the designer would soon be forgotten.

So essentially anonymous were the originators of these fascinating structures that at the height of their popularity towards the end of the century it was possible to buy all the necessary parts for a pier straight out of an ironfounder's catalogue. By this time no self-respecting seaside town could call itself a resort if it had no pier, an attendant collection of kiosks, shelters, pavilions and, of course, a bandstand. Brass bands were an essential part of the holiday scene even before pleasure piers were thought of (the Gloucestershire Militia was permanently stationed at Brighton so that its band could entertain the Prince Regent), and the need for shelters on the English coast is obvious.

33

Right
The pier, Penarth. In the early stages of their development piers were rather bare structures providing a platform for promenaders and a landing for steamers. This view of Penarth, with its entrance gates and kiosks and small platforms illustrates very clearly what such piers were like before the addition of the now familiar superstructures of pavilions, amusement arcades etc. Note the weighing machine

Middle
Margate Aquarium and Marine Polytechnic, 1876. A combination of brick and cast-iron which is as self-assertive as a railway terminus. It is buildings such as these which, whatever their stylistic deficiencies, give immense character to both British and Continental resorts and which are now so often replaced with characterless blocks devoid of any feature other than mere size. The Victorians understood and responded to scale

Bottom
Hastings pier at the beginning of the century. The uncluttered deck admirably expresses the concept of the promenade pier and the kiosks are among the best of their kind

The original purpose of piers was however to cater for the needs of the passenger boats which increased rapidly in number from the first decades of the century. Margate had a landing pier which was destroyed by a storm in 1808. It was replaced by one designed by Rennie and built at a cost of £100,000. This was at a time when cross channel passengers were still being disembarked at Brighton by rowing boats from ship to pebbly shore. Something, obviously, had to be done about this and the famous Chain Pier at Brighton was the result. Although built primarily as a landing stage it incorporated many of the features which were to become essential parts of any promenade pier.

Suspension bridges were among the many wonders of the age (Telford's Menai Bridge had been opened to traffic in 1826) and it was natural that this method of construction should be considered for the new pier at Brighton. A certain Captain Brown, RN, a pioneer in the field, was commissioned to execute the design, and the work was completed and opened to the public in 1823. It was built of wood and iron, wood being used mainly for the supports in order to withstand buffeting both from the sea and from boats. A series of towers supported the suspension chains which were anchored into the rock of the cliff. At the seaward end, some 350 yards from the entrance, passengers to and from the boats reached the landing stage by way of stairways from a platform. The prototype of all seaside piers had been built. Along its deck were shelters; souvenir shops and entertainments (including a *camera obscura*) occupied the bases of the supporting towers.

Within a few years piers were sprouting all round the coast. Scarborough's West Pier (strictly a harbour wall) was built in 1826, and by 1830 the pier that was destined to become the longest ever built was started at Southend. By this date even humble Walton-on-the-Naze thought fit to join in. Travel by road was still something of a nightmare and the railways were in their infancy, so the provision of a pier was as important to the potential prosperity of a seaside town as the opening of its railway station.

Birnbeck Pier, Weston-super-Mare. A print from a souvenir album showing the pier as originally constructed for use as a landing stage

Below
The Palace Pier, Brighton, at the turn of the century, unashamedly proclaiming itself 'The finest pier in the world'. This is the traditional pier at the climax of its development and as such one of the finest architectural expressions of the holiday spirit ever produced. It is difficult to believe that this complex of buildings has survived so many decades of battering by the often tempestuous seas of the English Channel

PALACE PIER, BRIGHTON, SHOWING NEW ENTRANCE.
THE FINEST PIER IN THE WORLD.   NO. 1.

A view from a Rock's Cabinet seaside souvenir album published just over a century ago. It shows the uninhibited use of landscape features to exploit the qualities of the situation

What is more, if the pier were municipally owned the revenues, as well as sea-borne visitors, were to the benefit of the town. Until the outbreak of the Second World War paddle boats were able to rival the railways for holiday traffic between London and the resorts on the east and south coasts. Lingering memories of *The Royal Daffodil* and similar vessels still evoke visions of pre-war holidays and day trips to the sea for thousands of Londoners. Although boats loaded with eager holidaymakers no longer leave Tower Pier on regular schedules (northwards to Southend, Clacton and Felixstowe or south along the Kent coast), Clacton and Margate piers still accommodate boats on cross channel day trips to Calais.

Iron, which was such a satisfactory material for the main structure of the pier, was less suitable for the actual landing stage, both because of its liability to break under impact and because of the need to allow for tidal changes. Wood was therefore used more frequently for these outer structures, and the contrast between the delicacy of ironwork and the robust sturdiness of wood is well displayed in pier construction. A particularly fine example is the landing stage attached to the end of Clevedon pier where a tidal range of 40 feet had to be allowed for. The original pier, built in 1869 from factory-made components assembled on the site, stretches 850 feet into the Bristol Channel to provide for the steamers which plied between resorts on the Somerset and Devonshire coasts and the towns of South Wales. At Weston-super-Mare the small island of Birnbeck was utilised in the construction of the boat pier serving the Channel steamers. The tidal race, however, posed considerable problems, and the cost in 1867 was nearly £70,000. The structure was soon put to use offering attractions to patrons other than intending passengers, and a toll of twopence was collected at the entrance. By this time the pattern for a typical pier was clearly established. Ward Lock's *Red Guide* described Birnbeck Pier as follows: 'The Pier proper has a length of 1,100 feet, and is 20 feet wide. A small line of rails runs down the middle for the conveyance of luggage to the steamers. On the island are large refreshment and waiting rooms, a waterchute, a switchback railway, swings and other delirious delights'.

Where nature had so fortunately provided Birnbeck Island other piers had to make their own, and the seaward platform with its large pavilion and variety of kiosks, shelters, bandstand or lifeboat house was a necessary component. One of the most striking examples is the nearby Grand Pier at Weston, built in 1903-04. Surmounted by a collection of domes of varying shape, encompassed by an iron balcony and suitably embellished it included a main hall seating 2,000, an outside bandstand (around which the audience were protected from the weather by canvas screens), shops and kiosks. In order to allow for the necessary height of the main deck the entrance to the Grand Pier was sloped upwards from the promenade between two small and delightfully unselfconscious pavilions. As with most piers the main deck between the entrance and the platform at the seaward end was clear of any superstructures other than wind screens, allowing maximum space for promenaders out to enjoy the sea air.

It is easy to overlook the fact that after providing landing stages for boats one of the main functions of piers when they were first built was to provide a seaward promenade from which to view the coastline. The view inland from a pierhead was a major attraction, and remains so in most cases, particularly at night. The addition of shelters along the length of the deck (as at Clacton) and of a variety of amusement arcades, dance halls, swimming pools and other attractions came later. The Victorians displayed an inordinate fascination for viewpoints and would go to great lengths to see a panoramic view. What better place then for the unadventurous to enjoy the advantages of a ship at sea, without the attendant perils or discomforts, than a walk to the end of the pier? In order to make the enterprise pay tollbooths were installed at the entrances and these, with their familiar turnstiles

The Victoria Promenade, Ilfracombe. Cast-iron was fully exploited in buildings such as this and provided an excellent setting for the exotic plants so loved by our great grandparents. Children were dressed as miniature adults and expected to behave accordingly, even at the seaside

Below
Bangor. The pattern of slender iron against the moving surface of water, the most successful architectural expression of the seaside spirit. This pier was built as a landing stage and still has an uncluttered promenade deck

Whitby. One of the many 'Gipsy Smiths'

Below
Brighton. Entwined cast-iron serpents typical of the inventive frivolity of pier design

and centre gateways (now for prams and pushchairs but originally more often for Bath chairs and other invalid carriages) are still a standard feature. Often the original buildings survive, giving a foretaste of the delights offered beyond the barrier. Sometimes these have been replaced by later and less agreeable structures, as at Lytham St Annes where the shabby but delightful pier is approached through a redbrick and half-timbered entrance. The latter gives no suggestion of the fanciful onion domes, complex roofs and brightly painted cast-iron trimmings of the pavilions at the seaward end, where the gaiety of the architecture even spreads to the coastguard hut projecting from the pierhead.

Whether or not the Brighton Pavilion had anything to do with subsequent pier design would be hard to prove, but a preference for vaguely oriental styles is undeniable. This is seen to its greatest advantage in the entrance tollbooths and the pierhead pavilions of the older piers, although overall designs changed surprisingly little over forty years or more. The most noticeable change has been a gradual tendency to add more and more buildings at each end of the pier, and to erect shelters or windbreaks along the length of the deck.

Clacton pier, a case in point, originally had an uninterrupted deck along which the only features shown in early prints were two boat davits similar to those used for lifeboats on board ship. Even the entrance appears to have been clear of buildings. Postcards from the turn of the century show the same uncluttered promenade but seats had been installed in small platforms projecting over the water; a few huts, including a shooting gallery, appeared at the entrance. The considerable developments at Clacton, which include the Blue Lagoon dance hall, 'dodgems', the 'Steel Stella' switchback ride, the childrens' railway, 'Hall of Mirrors', swimming pool, Helter Skelter and (at one time) a zoo, nearly all took place between the wars. This was when the impact of day trippers, in cars or by train from Liverpool Street, together with the building of Butlin's holiday camp, changed the whole

THE O____A___ ___STING

ROYAL GIPSY

We journey through
this world but once
& have short time to stay
whatever good I can do
had best be done to-day
For such another golden
chance you may wait
in vain Now is the time
because I shall not
pass this way
again.

Over half a century
of continued practice
in the art of palmistry
as enabled me to make
new discoveries & will
I trust add to the
value & completeness
of my work

PLEASE WALK IN

PLEASE WALK IN

NOW
OPEN
GIPSY SMITH

STEP INSIDE
AND HAVE
YOUR HAND READ
BY THE FAMOUS
___

Seaside souvenirs. Miscellaneous wooden objects with transfer prints showing typical seaside scenes

Below
A ribbon plate with gold and blue decoration and a transfer print of Cleethorpes pier. Cleethorpes and Blackpool were two of the most popular resorts available to the nineteenth century inhabitants of the industrial West Riding. Cheap souvenir china such as this, usually produced in Germany, survives in vast quantities, suggesting the lasting attractions of piers and similar features as symbols of the seaside holiday

character of the town. During the Second World War the centre of the pier was blown out (in order to obstruct an invasion) but fortunately it has been re-instated. The interesting ovoid pavilion at the seaward end of Clacton Pier appears to have been part of the original design, and it housed for very many years the typical pierrot shows and other recently defunct entertainments.

Most of the older piers had similarly modest beginnings and passing years have left them with pleasant encrustations of buildings of various kinds on the superstructure. Early souvenir pictures show the Victoria Pier at Blackpool with a line of rectangular booths on small side platforms. The entrance, as at Weston-super-Mare, slopes upwards and the fanciful little tollhouses must have been added later. These could not be bettered as visible symbols of the seaside spirit. Their onion domes, equally reminiscent of Tyrolean churches or eastern temples, are exotic visions on this exposed northern coast. Their roofs, incredibly complex for such small buildings, are surmounted by vanes and picked out in cast-iron ornamentation. Even the walls are panelled and faceted. The gates and gate pillars, although echoing the same mood, are ponderous by comparison. The pierhead pavilion displayed the same abandoned approach to architectural styles and was almost as successful.

Even Brighton's Palace Pier had nothing to compare with the Blackpool Victoria Pier entrance kiosks, but it did have a collection of ornately useless iron arches, both at the entrance and at intervals along the deck, which made a major contribution to its success as holiday architecture. Hastings, although less complex, had one typical octagonal kiosk with an extended roof and its own diminutive dome. No pier it would seem was complete without at least one such structure and many delightful examples survive. Bangor, which was primarily a steamer pier stretching two-thirds of the way across the Menai Strait, has one at the entrance flanking a cumbersome but highly ornamental set of heavy iron gates. These latter are in complete contrast to the

Brighton Aquarium, from a wooden souvenir

CE HALL, GRAND AQUARIUM, BRIGHT

modern, functional but totally unattractive tubular rails which protect the edge of the road leading up to the pier, evidence of changing attitudes to seaside landscape over the century.

Late nineteenth century views of pier entrances give a fair indication not only of the popular delights offered to holidaymakers, but also of some of the ingredients of life of the period. Clacton advertised 'Popular Concerts' in the Pavilion and 'Hot and Cold Sea Water'. At Hastings a Viennese band gave daily performances. The entrance to the Central Pier at Blackpool carried a placard announcing ' 2 Quadrille Bands play for Dancing on the Pier Head and Centre Platform . . . Open Air Concerts . . . and Daily Central Pier Collegians Entertainment'. In addition the buildings were in danger of being swamped by boards advertising several cures for headache, Sames Pianos, Boots the Chemists and 'Bovril, King in the Kitchen'.

Restraint or good taste have never been the characteristics of pier design. It is doubtful if many people take much notice of strange details or exotic forms used as motifs. It is the overall effect of freedom from normal restraints and standards which is so important. The really amazing thing is that all this was achieved in a location where it was necessary to withstand the forces of nature at their harshest and where they could exert their most constant destructive effect.

Iron, both wrought and cast, steel and wood were all used in their appropriate places and, although many piers suffered damage or destruction (the most recent casualty being Clevedon) the state of most of them is a tribute to the engineering skill of their designers and builders. The greatest hazard to the safety of a pier was the storm-blown ship and much damage was caused by such vessels being driven against them. The risk was greatest along the north-east coast where a succession of piers, including Saltburn, Redcar, Coatham and Scarborough, were all severely damaged by ships. The impact of a loaded collier out of control in a gale could, and sometimes did, carry away large sections of a pier. Coatham was cut in two by a ship in 1898 after only 25 years of existence and never replaced. Even the south coast was not immune, Worthing pier having been almost completely demolished by a storm in 1913. Such was the need for a pier in a resort of this kind that it was immediately rebuilt and subsequently considerably enlarged.

The Brighton Chain Pier was original in its construction but not unique. An elegant suspension pier was built at Seaview in the Isle of Wight in 1880, the curved decks of which were carried by wire ropes hung from four supporting towers. The more straightforward arrangement of piles driven through the sand was followed almost universally elsewhere and this gives most piers a dual character. The understructure of piles of varying thicknesses, placed at varying intervals and connected by a lattice of slender rods, creates a landscape which in itself is as typical of the seaside as the superstructure's pavilions, domes and ornament. One of the greatest pleasures from walking along many a foreshore is the changing pattern of black lines and bright shapes created by the understructure of a pier seen silhouetted against the sea or shining wet sand, a pleasure that is lost in wooden structures or some more recent concrete examples. Most of the older metal piers were supported on a forest of piles but a splendid exception to this rule was the pier at Clevedon which resembled an elegant visually flimsy bridge. The supports were tall and graceful, with delicately pierced spandrels where the ironwork of the legs spread to meet the deck. The crossed and horizontal ties, seen when looking along the length of the underside, were equally graceful and it is difficult to believe that such an apparently fragile structure survived over a century of buffeting by the sea before its recent partial collapse.

The delicate but austere understructure of a metal pile pier offers a fascinating contrast to the usually ornately vulgar superstructure. Beneath the deck the construction is severely functional, above it is the fanciful world of pleasure; a successful marriage of more unlikely partners would be hard to imagine.

The rigidly rectangular pattern of ironwork below gives place to curved rails, lacelike ornament, crestings and finials of intriguing complexity and a seeemingly inexhaustible wealth of decorative features. On the Palace Pier at Brighton the lampposts are held in the grip of entwined cast-iron snakes, and even the pier at Swanage which is little more than a landing stage has lampposts with ladder support-arms elaborated into strange winglike shapes. These must have come from an ironfounder's catalogue; they occur at a number of other resorts in various parts of the country.

The inventive originality displayed in the use of cast-iron ornament on the Palace Pier is unsurpassed. First opened to the public in 1899 at the very end of the golden age of pier building, the Palace Pier had taken nearly ten years to build and much was to be added later. It is considered by many to be the finest pleasure pier ever built. From the beginning every arch and every roofline was illuminated at night by electric light, and most of the original fittings still survive. At first the Palace Pier, which was built to replace the Chain Pier, followed the pattern of the latter in having a completely clear deck, but a pierhead platform with an ornate theatre was added and open by 1901. Within another ten years the theatre had been improved and a bandstand and winter-garden added. Over the entrance to the theatre was a large glass-fronted structure for use as 'a theatre in which drama can be acted for the purpose of being photographed by Cine-Camera'. Although this proved impracticable and the room is now used as a café it has a strong claim to being the first purpose-built film studio in the country.

The popularity of the pier between the wars continued to increase and 'Brighton Pier' became a universally known phrase with particular associations. Although, along with others, it was partly destroyed during the war it was renewed and re-opened by 1946. The winter-garden, reflecting changing tastes, is now a fun palace, with the usual proliferation of rides and amusements, but the tradition of pier usage remains unaltered. Pleasure boats still

Morecambe. The Palace and Aquarium: a sub-tropical wonderland on a northern Atlantic coast. Cast-iron, glass and the skills of late Victorian gardening combine to produce a fantastic exterior (right) and fascinating interior (below)

Right
**Worthing. Between-wars 'modern': note the square clockface and
predominance of horizontal banding**

Margate

Royan. Beach and casino nicely related

Far left
Souvenir plate showing the view landward from the end of Blackpool pier. The uncluttered deck is typical of the early days of piers

Left
Bexhill Kursaal, from an early postcard. Compare this with the respresentation beneath of the same subject in lithophanic china

Above
Picture from a two-inch square Victorian glass paperweight

Souvenir mug with lithophanic picture of Bexhill Kursaal

use the landing stages, anglers line the rails, old men still sit in the shelters staring out to sea and the young continue to shock them by their standards of dress and behaviour. Every year upwards of two million people pay a modest toll to enjoy its mixture of pleasures and excitements.

By the first decade of the present century the great age of pier building was at an end. Many existing structures were altered or enlarged but little new building was done. In England, at least, the pier remains an essentially Victorian object. In retrospect the consistency of pier design seems remarkable. Admittedly, variations on the long thin deck section, plus one or more platforms accommodating halls or pavilions of various kinds, would be difficult to envisage. But the persistence of onion domes and exotic styles translated freely into north European forms and adapted to a situation perched precariously above turbulent grey water is beyond explanation. Llandudno may have departed from normal practice to the extent of being Y-shaped, but its buildings are traditionally eastern in character, like some floating Buddhist temple cast ashore in North Wales. St Annes, built in 1885, had a Moorish Pavilion added in 1904 at a cost (together with an extension) of £30,000. From Blackpool to Hastings, and for something like half a century, piers had to be oriental. During the same period furious controversy raged over the correct style for a church or a town hall, but there were no doubts at all about piers.

It was not until the latter half of the present century that a major departure from this rule was made. The new pier at Scheveningen in Holland is in a distinctly contemporary style and with no trace of oriental influence. Although most modern architecture has an essentially international character with local identity a thing of the past, Scheveningen proves that a pier remains a unique architectural form. The 1,160 foot length of deck originally branched into three seaward platforms. These were curved and exploited changes of level to create an atmosphere like that on a cruise liner. At the farthest end a tower spirals skyward

and another stands near the entrance bearing advertising material. Following earlier precedents the pier was enlarged by the addition of a fourth 'island' in 1964. The main departure from precedent has been in the use of galvanised steel for most of the structural work. Whether the environment it has created will prove to be as lastingly attractive as the fripperies of the nineteenth century remains to be seen.

The north European coast has a number of pleasure piers, mostly similar to the English pattern and erected no doubt partly because of English influence. The Englishman abroad has always expected to be able to find a home from home at his chosen resort, as can be seen from the 'English teas' and 'fish and chips' of contemporary Calais and other Channel resorts, and the fact that these home-grown delights are now spreading to the Spanish coast and other package tour areas of the Mediterranean. The piers on the Belgian coast must owe their origin partly to the fact that the slightly more affluent or adventurous English holidaymakers of the turn of the century were choosing to cross the Channel as an alternative to sharing the resorts of the Sussex, Kent and Essex coast with the new influx of railway day trippers.

Popular entertainment demanded far more accommodation than could be provided on the pier or in the pier pavilion. Buildings were required to house all manner of diversions from straight theatrical performances to circuses, and many of these show the direct influence of pier construction or design. During the latter part of the nineteenth century one essential of any self-respecting resort was a winter-garden or similar building. No middle class villa was complete without its conservatory, and no seaside town was complete without its vastly enlarged public version of the same thing. Cast-iron and glass were the most important building materials and the influence of piers and of Paxton and his Crystal Palace is evident. The Victorian English understood and appreciated plants probably more than any other people in history and a display of luxuriant sub-tropical flora

Ramsgate. The art of overdoing it without going too far, so well done as to continue to function visually after more than half a century

Below
Clacton pier. The elegant original theatre at the seaward end

provided a background to many social activities. The winter-gardens in their heyday provided some of the finest examples of indoor gardening ever seen and their sad decline into the palm courts of the Edwardian or inter-war hotels is to be regretted.

In the nineteenth century it was an achievement to grow flowers or fruit out of season or beyond their natural habitat; the wonder of it was a source of popular enjoyment. Now that we are able to obtain fruit and flowers anywhere, at any time, we have lost much of the naïve pleasure of seeing growing things out of their proper contexts of time and place. The collecting of ferns or mosses from the sea damp rocks, of strange flowers for pressing, or of seaweeds for painting in watercolours was one of the joys of the family holiday. The winter-garden or the aquarium were an extension of the same interests and delights. In the glass and iron halls visitors could take morning coffee or afternoon tea, listen to a concert or see an exhibition. The artificial climate could be controlled and the holiday season extended.

The long season of the English seaside holiday came to an abrupt end at the outbreak of the First World War, and by the time peace and more settled conditions returned much of the old flavour had been lost, forgotten or superseded. The leisurely days of quadrille bands in the pavilion and genteel chamber music in the winter-garden were but symbols of a bygone age, lingering on only in the memory or provincial backwaters. The emergent new age was one of noise, of frenzied entertainment and of brash new styles and materials. At last cast-iron and the Brighton Pavilion were forgotten and something quite different began to appear.

Perhaps the most typical building of the period between the wars is the Blue Lagoon dance hall at the landward end of Clacton Pier. The very name conjures up the atmosphere of an era, and the original use of coloured glass in assorted rectangular panels is typical of the best entertainment architecture of a period which also produced the finest of the picture palaces. Glass and chrome were as typical of this age as cast-iron was of the late Victorian.

Brighton. The landing stage now used predominantly by anglers

Below
Brighton. Pier rhythm

53

Aerial view of the pier at Scheveningen, Holland, before construction of the fourth 'island'. The most imaginative of recent piers, planned to allow for further growth. Now that accommodation is no longer required for steamer berths the pier can begin to evolve new forms, as is evident in the design of the 'islands'

That it was not as widely used at the seaside was due to the fact that most of the necessary building had already been done and only comparatively small additions were required. The small pavilion halfway along Worthing Pier is a good example of this 'jazz style', complete to its square-faced clock. The latter is evidence of the way in which so called functional architecture was copied as a style without any understanding of its true nature. Entertainment architecture has always thrived on the absurd, and Worthing's pavilion is no exception.

Along with the jazz style, of which there are disappointingly few examples, there evolved a kind of heavy handed, angular municipal style, most frequently encountered built into cliff faces as at Margate. Having suffered the fate of other unfashionable styles and having been ignored for several decades, the municipal style can be seen at this distance in time as an important addition to the seaside landscape. The characteristic material is brick, sometimes painted or rendered, and the detailing is usually a coarsened version of 'post office Georgian'. In this case the caricature is usually better than the original. Considerable use is made of flat roofs as sun terraces and even at this late date cast-iron is occasionally employed for railings. Lampposts on brick plinths are another recurring feature, the lanterns being versions of a number of severely rectangular forms. These buildings must be among the last in which cast-iron was successfully used as a major decorative feature. An imaginative and purely speculative design for a cast-iron pier, published by Richard Sheppard in 1945, was, alas, never taken sufficiently seriously to be considered as the basis for an actual construction.

By the end of the 1930s the distinctions between vernacular and sophisticated architecture at the seaside were becoming increasingly blurred and the post-war styles which have temporarily destroyed regional identities had not taken over as disastrously as in subsequent decades. Most seaside buildings were designed either by municipal architects or by comparatively

Enamel notice at Salcombe, Devon. Such details make a major
contribution to seaside atmosphere but they are vulnerable to thoughtless
destruction

undistinguished professionals. The one major exception was the
De la Warr Pavilion built by Erich Mendelsohn at Bexhill in 1934.
This building is unique in English seaside architecture, a major
work of a leading architect of international repute.

Since the war a more appropriately lighthearted approach
has become apparent, particularly in Europe and America. The
casino on the seafront at Royan, rebuilt after the total devastation
of the war, is a good example. If this could be regarded as typical
then the immediate future might produce some exciting additions
to the seaside landscape. There are indications elsewhere that this
is beginning to happen.

Chapter 3

AMUSEMENTS

An early nineteenth century engraving of Punch and Judy

Ever since seaside resorts began to develop in the last century they have been obvious centres for all kinds of popular amusements. Many families would allow themselves the indulgence of a visit to the theatre or a turn on the slot machines at the seaside and then return home to an atmosphere in which such pleasures were frowned on, or out of reach for financial reasons. Among the attractions offered to the holidaymaker novelty has always had pride of place. Accordingly many forms of amusement which have now developed into universally accepted entertainments had their origins at the seaside. New delights for ear and eye, new sensations and if possible a suggestion of things ever so slightly naughty in the context of their day and age have challenged the designers of amusement machines and the impressarios of live shows alike. From pier theatre to Punch and Judy, for well over a century, many an inventive mind has responded to the challenge.

Among the more tantalising of these amusements, luring penny after penny into the seemingly bottomless collecting boxes of the showmen's machines, optical devices have led the way, until in recent years we have all become sated with the sensational and spectacular in moving pictures large and small. First the *camera obscura* delighted simple folk accustomed to even simpler pleasures. There was one on the Brighton Chain Pier in 1824, with its constantly moving microcosmic panorama of life outside. It depended only on the weather for its success, for on a dull day there was not enough light to penetrate the darkness of the booth in which the picture was displayed. It seems they have now disappeared from the seaside, but one remains on the Castle Hill in Edinburgh.

The Victorians were fascinated by optical effects and illusions and a number of devices which made use of the phenomenon known as persistence of vision were popular as toys or home entertainments. Pictures which were made to pass before the eye in such rapid succession as to become visually superimposed, and thus appearing to move, formed the basis of a number of inventive contraptions which by the end of the century had been developed into slot machines. Of these the one that proved to be the longest-lasting in its popularity (a few can still be found) was the mutoscope, better known as the 'What the Butler Saw' machine. The mild striptease which was the almost universal subject matter for these machines was a far more effective entertainment than the 'glamour' transparencies with which many of them have been replaced, for they appealed to the imagination and aroused an inquisitive excitement as to what happens next. The fact that 'what the butler saw' has become a stock phrase in the English language indicates how wide and consistent an appeal these machines had.

It is difficult to establish exactly when the machines first appeared but by the end of the last century they were well established as part of any seaside entertainment. The earliest examples worked for a halfpenny, but were soon adapted to the penny standard. Such titles as 'French Can-Can', 'The Hula Dancer' and 'Death Dive' indicate that a taste for sex and suspense is nothing new in popular entertainment though means of gratifying it may vary somewhat.

The popularity of seaside slot machines brought the 'Fun Houses' and amusement arcades in which they were installed. These have always had close links with the world of the fairground and with fairground families, many of whom settled into the amusement arcade business. One such family are the Barrons of Great Yarmouth, manufacturers of slot machines (including what is claimed to be the first English machine) as well as managers of a variety of entertainments. They were the first to show cinematograph performances in music halls in London and they also established one of the earliest seaside amusement halls, known as the Jubilee Exhibition, in Great Yarmouth. This contained among other delights a Jungle Rifle Range, Hand-Reading by a Lady Expert, Mechanical Models, Electrical Engraving and a Fancy Bazaar. Living exhibits included The Harem and a giant doorman.

A Victorian wood engraving of children at the seaside. Children's pleasures have not changed but fortunately their clothes have

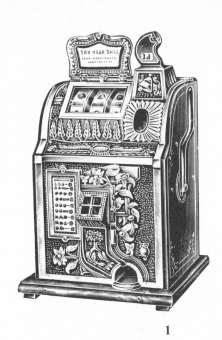

1

2

3

4

A representative selection of slot
machines from the advertising literature
of a firm of suppliers in the 1930s. On
the right is a 'mutoscope' or 'what the
butler saw' machine. Each of these
machines typifies the contents of the
amusement arcades from the First
World War until well into the 1950s.

5

Listening to the band. A popular seaside entertainment for nearly a century

Band of the Royal Marines on the Hoe, Plymouth

Below
Tennis at Weymouth. A typical scene of the late 1920s or 1930s. The popularity of tennis approached a mania and any hotel which could find the space for its own tennis court found it an immense advantage in attracting guests

Bottom
A 'clucking hen' which delivered a metal egg containing a trinket.

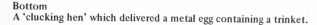

WEYMOUTH. Greenhill Gardens Tennis Courts.

When the Jubilee Exhibition was burnt down in 1901 an eyewitness described how 'Beautiful Marie, the Giant School Girl', on show at the rear of the building, had a miraculous escape, leaving the building in the nick of time and taking her pet canary with her. The hall was rebuilt after the fire and is still a feature of the Yarmouth seafront, although another early Yarmouth landmark, the metal observation tower, was demolished because of subsidence.

The history of the slot machine is virtually unrecorded. It is a subject that reveals an incredible inventiveness both in design and nomenclature. Early photographs of Barron's works taken at the turn of the century show that this inventiveness has been a characteristic of the trade from the beginning. The first machine delivered for one penny a fortune card giving information according to the colour of the subject's hair and eyes; it was made in two and four draw models. Other machines of the period displayed their fairground origins. For a halfpenny, one invited punters to see 'how high you can blow the elevator' on a model house. Another halfpenny machine was a version of the punchball known as 'The Blacksmith'; the selection also included a 'New Auto Piano', precursor of the juke box. The origins of the one-armed bandit or fruit machine can be found in 'The Elk', manufactured by the Mills Novelty Company of Chicago, which first appeared in the arcades in about 1904. This machine had spinning coloured bands which lined up to give a win, as in the fruit machine. The name was derived from an elk's head cast into the casing.

The names of many later machines were as imaginative as the objects themselves. One of the oldest suppliers in the business, Bolland's Amusement Machine Supply Company, listed more than 200 different machines around their 1930s notepaper, including such exotic and evocative names as 'Silver Flash', 'Electric Allwins', 'Mother Shipton', 'English Beauties', 'Krac Shot', 'Knickerbocker', 'Circle of Pleasure' and 'Conqueror's Flag'. The

Most of the development of Cromer took place during the Edwardian period. Women were beginning to show themselves publicly taking part in outdoor pursuits such as golf. Although the dresses may have hampered play they were the forerunner of the ultra-short shorts, bikinis and miniskirts of recent years

Below
Donkey rides: one of the oldest of seaside attractions and still very popular. The strings of donkeys with their coloured rosettes and fanciful names enliven most English beaches

WE SIX AT BLACKPOOL.

The Invalid's Walk, Bournemouth. A superb example of the plates contained in souvenir albums of the late nineties, before the general introduction of the halftone block. Apart from its delightful draughtsmanship (reminiscent of the work of Henri Rousseau, who was active at the time) the picture shows how much the Victorians appreciated and used foliage. The name is indicative of the origins of many resorts as places to visit for the sake of one's health

Bolland company's records cover the period from 1880 to the outbreak of war in 1939 and thus represent an almost complete history of the amusement machine. Distribution of the nineteenth century machines was divided between seaside resorts and railway stations, and they were supplied on a 50 per cent profit-sharing basis. The firm's collector was the ultimate in railway commuters, travelling from station to station emptying the machines and waiting for the next local to carry him onward. A pause at the seaside must have offered welcome relief. Early postcards of piers nearly all show some slot machines at strategic points. The machines were so profitable that by 1904 the owner of the firm had bought himself a 200 acre farm, and so popular had they become that they began to appear in the pages of Gamage's catalogues from as little as £2.50 each.

In the years between the wars the machines, still familiar though fast disappearing, began to fill the piers and arcades of practically every seaside town in the country. The trade was exporting large numbers and also importing from Germany and elsewhere. The most familiar and well remembered import was probably the chicken machine, or 'Clucking Hen', which delivered a coloured metal egg filled with 'swag' (charms, small toys, rings and the like). At one time more than five million of these eggs were being supplied each year, but Hitler switched the manufacturers over to weightier matters and the supply dried up. The same firm which marketed the chicken machines was also supplying more than five million fortune cards a year in the 1930s.

Most of the machines in the coastal towns were then either games, such as the metal footballers in their tiny knitted jerseys, fortune tellers, tableaux ('The Haunted Graveyard', 'Madame Guillotine' and similar spine-chilling scenes) or those which delivered small presents in various ways. The straightforward gambling machine was in the minority. Its threatened takeover in recent years has been halted by the Gaming Laws and a new generation of amusement machines is likely to result. A few of the

St Jean-de-Luz. Beach games for children and adults

Below
Clock golf on the hotel lawn. One of the genteel sports which gained immense popularity among middle class holidaymakers in the thirties. The immaculately kept gardens, uniformed waiters and equipment for afternoon tea on the lawn were all part of the essential provision for clients from the already overcrowded cities

outhport Water Chute and Maxim Flying Machine

Southport. The obviously popular water chute and flying machine attracting crowds of spectators as well as braver participants

der machines, including the ubiquitous cranes with their lippery and well-wedged prizes, have been temporarily saved om the scrapyard.

By the outbreak of war in 1939 the arcades housed a mixture f the traditional machines and the newer electrical devices, ainly updated versions of the pintable, with flashing lights and uzzers and numbers indicated on an illuminated glass panel, creen-printed with various pop art devices and pictures. Many musement halls retain their traditional character though the ccent is increasingly on prize money and less on novelty. The ominant machines of the late 1960s were the fruit machines and range based on the idea of running pennies down a slot or incline o form a pile until eventually one penny pushed the others over ie side for a win. Perhaps we have become too sophisticated to njoy the older style of novelty machine with its cheap (usually riental) gifts, but there can be no doubt that the element of hildish wonder, so characteristic of the early machines, has isappeared.

Gone, too, are the sounds which indicated 'all the fun of the air'. Fairground organs are now collectors' items, like the various inds of musical box which were their amusement arcade quivalent. At the beginning of the century coin-operated organs vere as necessary to a pier as to a pub. Many were made by talians working in the Hatton Garden area. Drums or rollers ould be changed to bring the tunes up to date, and in the twenties he job of marking out these rollers to play the latest tunes was one in his spare time by a Sussex clergyman named Wintle. German polyphones, working from large revolving discs, were mported during the same period. They were operated by a lockwork motor which earned as much as two shillings with one rind-up. When juke boxes were first introduced in the mid-thirties he clockwork motors from many of the polyphones were used to rive working-model tableaux such as the 'Execution' or the Haunted Graveyard'. The distinctive sound of the amusement

arcade has now been drowned in the universal pop music which, as 'muzak', has now spread to supermarkets and even office buildings. Along the beaches of Surfers' Paradise in Australia pop is played continuously from loudspeakers along the shore, interspersed inevitably with advertisements.

The virtual takeover by electronics of the noises of popular entertainment has immensely increased the range of sounds, and many of the new ones are peculiarly suitable to such situations. So also are many of the plastic and fibreglass materials developed since the war. They have made possible vast new inventions in the amusement world, such as can be seen and enjoyed at the Pleasure Beach at Blackpool. This place comes as near as anywhere to the creation of a 'fun environment' and it is particularly successful at night when the use of light and sound accentuates the deliberately evoked mood of fantasy, so successful in loosening both the inhibitions and the small change of the customers. It is a world away from the old style fairground which is still essentially Victorian or Edwardian in character (as can be seen, for example, in the superb 'Galloping Horses' on Walton Pier), yet it shares a common basis of novelty and excitement and the attempt to take us, however momentarily, 'out of this world'. New materials and new architectural and constructional idioms are quickly and skilfully recognised and adapted to the cause of entertainment. The pleasure beach is one of the few places in which such devices as the chair lift or the monorail can be experienced for their novelty alone. The fun has gone out of travelling for most people but in such places as this and in one or two holiday camps you can enjoy a journey which takes you nowhere and brings you back to the point from which you started for nothing more than the mere sensation of travelling.

Most of us manage for most of the time to suppress our sense of wonder in case we are thought to be childish, but such places as the pleasure beach allow us an opportunity to become children again. Giant animals inhabit a huge 'Noah's Ark'; we can enjoy the

Left

Ilfracombe. Capstone Parade from the east end

Right

The Water Park at Worthing. A typical example of a nineteenth century seaside park. In the evenings, after hotel dinners had been served, these parks would be filled with holidaymakers strolling in their best clothes. The attractions of water and ornamental fowl have long been recognised

Middle right

The waterfall, Blackpool South Shore, before the First World War. A not too successful attempt to simulate a mountain landscape in Lancashire. Such features as these, successful or not, are essential to any seaside resort, providing something unusual to talk about long after the holiday finishes

Bottom right

Rustic work in Grove Park, Weston-super-Mare. This delightfully intimate piece of garden design is typical of the best of small scale municipal park planning. Although catering for mass use it retains the quality of an enclosed garden, full of secret places

Below

Seaside lettering

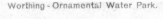

Worthing - Ornamental Water Park.

THE WATERFALL, SOUTH SHORE, BLACKPOOL.

sensation of being flung around, hurled into space, plunged down chutes into water or lured along dark passages into fascinating but frightening unknowns. We can play games as spacemen or lumberjacks, and inhabit a make believe world of plastic domes and fantastic buildings loaded with all the gimmickry known to architecture. An excellent example of the imaginative use of contemporary architectural idioms in an exciting but nonetheless meaningless way is the Blackpool 'Log Flume'; but here the whole Pleasure Beach, detail by detail, creates its own real but faintly unbelievable world.

When Blackpool's illuminations are switched on the atmosphere of the Pleasure Beach and Funfair is successfully extended for several miles along the whole seafront, transforming buildings which by day are most ordinary into one great landscape of fun and fantasy. Since the invention of the electric light the use of illuminations has been part of the seaside tradition, but never has it been carried to such magnificent extremes as in present day Blackpool. It matters little that many of the designs are intrinsically banal. The total effect is what matters and this is undeniably magnificent. The crowning glory of the whole fantastic exercise is the fleet of seaside trams, dressed up as steam engines, Mississippi paddle steamers and other unlikely objects. It is a transformation that converts a northern seafront into something approaching our childhood notion of fairyland; it must rank among the major achievements of environmental design. Incredibly, it is seen at its best when rain is sweeping in from the sea and the roads are packed with the cars and coaches of thousands of visitors, when coloured lights merge and reflect off the constantly moving pattern of wet car roofs and shining road surfaces.

Such places as the Blackpool Pleasure Beach mark a halfway stage between traditional entertainments with their origins in the fairground and the totally planned and organised environments made possible by recent developments in plastics, electronics and

The Sanatorium, Bournemouth. The traditionsl functions of the 'health resort' continued well into this century and only began their gradual decline with the conquest of tuberculosis.

Below
Some seaside attractions of the turn of the century: donkey rides, fishing trips, bathing, sitting in the sun and having your photograph taken (note the portable darkroom). Equipment lined up to await the seasonal rush at Broadstairs, c.1900

Clacton pier before the addition of most of the superstructure. The two slot machines are early examples. This view vividly illustrates the purpose of a pier as a place from which to see the shore, as from a boat.

Below
Stalls on the beach at Southsea, c.1900

Ramsgate. Real 'pop' art: plastic decoration transforming an otherwise undistinguished building

he programming of sound and light effects. These offer prospects at least as potentially exciting as the piers of the last century, and already some progress has been made in this direction. An interesting example is the fun palace called 'The Fifth Dimension' at Girvan in Ayrshire. This is built up from a number of interchangable spherical and tubular units in plastic. The exterior is less interesting than the interior, but once inside the visitor is subjected to a series of changes designed to stimulate all the senses except smell. The lighting changes constantly both in colour and intensity, and as the explorer in this dream chamber feels his way from point to point the surfaces he touches and on which he stands vary in texture from smooth to abrasive, warm to cold. Even the floor changes suddenly from concrete to sponge. Assailed by electronically produced sounds, the visitor is thus completely contained in an environment totally designed for its purpose. Costing some £10,000, 'The Fifth Dimension' indicates a totally new line of future development for seaside amusements. Unfortunately in its present form it is designed almost entirely for its interior effect and thus its impact on the surrounding landscape is less successful than earlier forms. Nevertheless it does prove that the development of seaside amusements is far from being a phenomenon of the past and that modern technology, suitably handled, has a lot to offer in the field of fun and games.

The fun palaces and fairgrounds have changed radically only in the past decade in which, paradoxically, the older forms of amusement have once more become objects of interest. The enthusiasms surrounding steam railway engines have spread to include fairground engines and fairground machinery just as the last of these were being withdrawn. At the seaside most of the older, spectacular amusements have disappeared but a few remain. The Blackpool Tower, built in 1894, still dominates the seafront and is the centrepiece of the most spectacular collection of seaside entertainments in Britain, but the enormous revolving wheel which stood beside the tower and is prominent in all the early

Below
Scarborough. Funfair: plastic signs and neon lights

Bottom
Southport illuminations in the early 1900s. The marvels of electric lighting were used to enhance the attractions of seaside resorts long before they were universally applied to town lighting. Their attractions must have been infinitely greater in the dayswhen they were a novelty and when many homes were still lit by gas

souvenirs and postcards of the resort has unfortunately gone. The equally exciting and prominent water chute at Southport, built in 1892 as part of a major scheme which included the lake into which it projected its riders, was demolished in 1922. Few of the remaining rides or amusement machines have either the scale or the naïve appeal of these earlier examples, although the 'Steel Stella' switchback on Clacton Pier manages to appeal to the same sensations after a run of nearly 40 years.

Diversions of a milder kind have always had an important place in the range of holiday facilities, and these proliferated in the period between the wars. Traditional donkey rides (still a favourite for small children) were supplemented by a variety of activities ranging from obstacle golf to boating and paddling pools. Models of all kinds proved their fascination in the same period, and model villages and model railways took their place among the necessary provisions of the leading or aspiring resorts. During the thirties catering for children became a dominant influence on the holiday landscape for the first time. The donkeys and the Punch and Judy shows have retained their popularity in spite of the more sophisticated offerings of the post-war years, and the same can be said of the swings, see-saws, the manually propelled roundabouts and the climbing frames without which no European beach is now complete. The children's beach clubs which are such an attractive and widespread feature on the continent have failed to spread to England, possibly because of different attitudes to family life.

The thirties are now full of nostalgia as the generation which experienced those years as children now moves into middle age. When Britain's Fred Perry dominated Wimbledon a craze for tennis spread through the land, and family hotels with large lawns were quick to turn them into tennis courts. Clock golf sufficed in less spacious surroundings. Provision for both golf and tennis had to be made on a proper scale, usually by the local authority. Golf, even for the ladies, had featured among the attractions of the forward-looking resorts since the end of the previous century.

THE ILLUMINATIONS, SOUTHPORT.

'Steel Stella'. Clacton pier. Children's train in foreground

Below
Margate. The fairground has longstanding links with the seaside, and many of the best seaside amusements are designed and operated by families descended from generations of travelling showmen. The Margate fairground is one of the largest and best

The pleasure garden was an essential ingredient of the seaside landscape. Every resort had its parks and gardens, often created with great ingenuity. These are still largely unrecognised although contemporary municipal gardening owes them a great deal. Rocks and exotic plants were used in abundance with a great appreciation of the forms and colours of foliage

ROCK WALK, TORQUAY.

For those who considered themselves to be above the common thrills and delights of the fairground or amusement arcade, and for whom the active sports were too energetic, other forms of amusement had to be provided. Scenic walks and gardens were an obvious solution, and it is fortunate that much of the original work in providing these was done during the later years of the nineteenth century. The Victorian genius for gardening has been insufficiently recognised, as has the English municipal garden and public park. The two combined to great effect at the seaside, where many great garden landscapes now pass almost unnoticed so accustomed are we to their presence. True to Victorian traditions the cultivation of exotic and unlikely plants took pride of place, particularly along the Devon and Cornish coasts where a fortunate combination of soil and climate made sub-tropical gardening a possibility. The achievements of the indoor winter-gardens and palm and fern houses were transferred outdoors with great skill.

Walking through well stocked and beautifully landscaped gardens, visiting the glasshouses and feeding the strange-plumed birds on the inevitable ornamental lake were regarded as pleasant and civilised ways of enjoying a holiday. So too was the vanity of parading one's best clothes after hotel dinner on a summer's evening. Where rocks or natural cliff faces existed they were exploited to the full as rock gardens, often enhanced by artificial waterfalls, grottoes or rustic caves and arbours. The Chines at Bournemouth are good examples of the way in which natural features could be used to scenic advantage. Late nineteenth century illustrations of the Invalids' Walk in Bournemouth show how appreciative the Victorians were of foliage, in contrast to our contemporary passion for floral colour which is no doubt inspired to some extent by the rapid spread of colour photography. The name Invalids' Walk reminds us that the Victorian resorts relied for their prosperity not so much on families with children as upon affluent retired gentlefolk and wealthy invalids who came to the

'The Enchanted Grotto', Blackpool. The Blackpool illuminations have achieved an unrivalled reputation and attract vast crowds. They also successfully extend the 'season' and thus help to overcome one of the most difficult problems faced by British resorts. The illumination obliterate the solidity of buildings and create a new landscape of light and colour. Their success (due in part to their exciting vulgarity) shows what can be done to create an effect of fun and pleasure which still has an almost universal appeal

seaside not for holidays but for health. Sanatoria were a conspicuous feature of most resorts until the middle of the present century and many private nursing homes are still to be found in them.

Bath chairs have been replaced by mini-cars and motor-scooters and prosperity no longer depends on the patronage of a declining race of monied invalids and retired colonial administrators. Contemporary amusements have to appeal to families accustomed to the professionalism of television production and to a teenage generation enjoying more money and more freedom than at the same age their parents would have dreamed possible. Many a Lancashire teenager spends more on a week in Blackpool than his parents do for a fortnight in a Spanish resort, and the Golden Mile with its stalls, kiosks and sideshows reflects a young, exciting, brash and colourful search for the new, the novel and the exotic. It is the old fairground updated (and up-priced) but still as infectiously appealing.

Chapter 4
HOTELS AND BOARDING HOUSES

Deal. A fascinating glimpse of the seafront from one of the alleyways which connect at right angles to the promenade. The period detail becomes coarser as it is more recent, culminating in the characterless ugliness of the standard grey parking restriction post of our own age

During the first few decades of the nineteenth century the character of many seaside towns and villages changed from that of either fashionable watering places for the nobility and gentry or working ports and fishing villages to that of family resorts. Many places had already changed beyond recognition as increasing trade and prosperity encouraged new building and attracted professional men able to build impressive houses in the fashionable Georgian style and, towards the end of the eighteenth century, the air of solid respectability which pervaded many small seaside towns, particularly along the south coast, was disturbed by an invasion of sophisticated society from London which brought with it a passion for the more superficial and showy architecture which we now admire and describe as Regency. The comfortable-looking redbrick Georgian boxes, well proportioned and pleasantly inoffensive, were too puritanical in their attention to good taste for the showy extrovert high society of the Regency period. When George III went to Weymouth in 1789 his arrival was to set in motion a conversion from quiet prosperity to fashionable elegance, and this was to be repeated to the point of caricature under the later influence of his profligate son.

The character of many of these Channel coast resorts remains to this day essentially as it was created in the half century or so before the arrival of the railways. The towns along the shore from the Medway ports to Dover are still Georgian in character behind their façades, and it is not difficult to find backstreets in Deal or Broadstairs which look like settings for an episode in a Dickens novel. The magnificence of the seafront architecture of Brighton and Hove, which in total is one of the great achievements of European culture, is overpoweringly Regency in its effect and although most of the buildings have been converted to other uses it is still essentially a mass of splendid apartments evoking the mannered society for which it provided such an admirable background. They are, perhaps, along with Bath, the finest stage sets in history.

Right
St Jean-de-Luz

Below
Sidmouth. The superb group of ornamental villas
at the western end of the short promenade

Budleigh Salterton. 'Cottage ornée' planted near the sea when this was beginning to be regarded as a desirable situation. Now the museum

Many of the late eighteenth century or early nineteenth century houses are now converted into hotels but the period of the custom-built hotel came later. The comparison between converted buildings of an earlier period and the hotels of the mid-Victorian age is interesting, for hotels not only produced a new architectural form but also revealed a whole range of long defunct social attitudes. The Royal Hotel at Deal is typical of the early period, associated more with coaching inns than seaside holidays. It is an unassuming building occupying an isolated position on the seafront between a line of mainly eighteenth century buildings facing sea and beach. Its plain but dignified façade is relieved only by a pedimented doorway surmounted by a vigorously carved and skilfully placed painted royal arms in wood. The solidity of its design, enlivened by the colour and gilt of heraldry, has a flavour of the roast beef of old England about it.

All along the coast, at least as far west as Weymouth, are terraces of Regency buildings now converted into hotels and holiday apartments. At last it has been recognised that much of their charm lies in their well bred frivolity and many owners have responded by painting them in a delightful range of chaste but exotic colours. The range of colour-fast paints, greater now than at any other time, has done much to reveal the appropriateness of these Regency buildings to their seaside setting. The flowing curves of crescents and serpentine streets (often following the lie of the land, as at Folkestone), the lacelike balconies with their curved or corrugated canopies, flights of steps up to front doors, or down to the areas for tradesmen and servants, painted cornices, and servants' rooms peeping through diminutive decorated windows on a high-pitched and much-chimneyed roof, these are the architectural forms and patterns which had already become seaside architecture before the beginning of the hotel era. Beneath their colourwash and behind their modern signs and tubs of pelargoniums they still say 'seaside' to most of us.

The change from private villa to hotel was soon to take

place. Along the seafront between the lower end of the High Street and the Cobb at Lyme Regis are some excellent examples of tile-hung, fretwork-porched private villas for upper middle class Victorian family holidays. At Sidmouth the villas of the gentry and nobility provide a textbook of changing tastes from Regency to mid-Victorian building. The Grand Duchess of Russia had a villa there, and behind the larger houses of such illustrious personages were the smaller ornamented cottages of those lower down the social scale. They show the transition from the elegant splendours of the Regency terraces to the italianate monuments to individual status so beloved of the Victorians. Both architecturally and socially they are far removed from their immediate precursors.

Undeniably, and some might add unfortunately, the beginning of the hotel era coincided with a period of monumental individuality in architecture rather than with one that sought unified effect in large scale planning. This was of course inevitable, a characteristic of that pride in individual prowess and success which made the whole nineteenth century achievement possible. It would be surprising if the men who built the railways, who sank their own and other people's fortunes in spectacular enterprises and responded heroically to the prospects opening before them in an heroic age, had chosen to express modest self-effacement in their architecture. The proprietors and entrepreneurs of the railway age could no more have commissioned the Regency terraces than they could have foreseen the eventual conquest of steam power by electric traction and the internal combustion engine.

The beginnings of hotel architecture can be seen in such examples as the Albion on the front at Broadstairs. This was described in 1816 as 'a new-built house, conveniently fitted up'; its name, displayed in robust sans serif letters incised across the front, conjures up just the right image. The classical name for Britain was so beloved of the Victorians that they used it liberally

Advertisement from an early Ward Lock's guide

for many of their finest creations: locomotives, the Albion Press, Albion Mills and so on. The Albion Hotel has the heavy Regency-inspired ornament so commonly seen on the rapidly disappearing architecture of Kensington, and it retains a balcony facing the sea. It is assertive where the true Regency buildings were elegant but it is nonetheless successful. For all its heavy mouldings it was a restrained version of what was to follow.

It would be near the truth to suggest that the railways were the influence most responsible for the forms taken by hotel architecture in the last century. Much has been written about the great metropolitan termini and the wrangling over gothic, classical or italianate styles for the massive hotels with which the railway companies inexplicably sought to hide the stupendous engineering achievements of the great train sheds, but surprisingly little has been said of the activities of the same companies when their lines eventually reached the seaside. All round the coast of England stand the smaller but equally typical examples of railway hotels, many of them still as dominant in their settings as they were originally intended to be. Some outlived their parent and still serve as hotels long after the railway which brought them into being has been closed and its stations demolished.

Of these seaside railway hotels the Great Eastern at Harwich is a fair example. It now serves as the town hall and even in this capacity its monumental size and character are out of keeping with its setting. When the hotel was built in 1864 Harwich was still predominantly a small working port relying for its livelihood on an estuary harbour with some inland traffic and on its naval associations. The few buildings of any interest could be seen easily within a morning's walk and its potential as a family resort, as history has proved but as the railway failed to envisage, was severely limited. The railway companies were, as usual in this connection, wildly optimistic and they planted on the quayside a monstrous four storey italianate pile which after the passing of more than a century still looks out of place. The railway lines ran

MEDLEY" HYDROPATHIC ESTABLISHMENT,
GAR ROAD, BIRKDALE PARK.

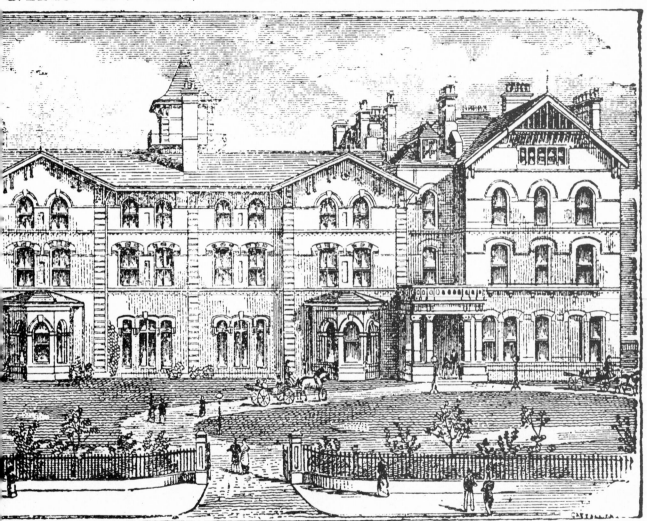

THE NEW

TURKISH BATH,

WITH

SWIMMING
BATH

ATTACHED,

is one of the

FINEST in the

KINGDOM,

AND IS

FREE

TO

RESIDENTS

IN THE

Establishment.

ysician—Dr. F. A. ERNEST BARNARDO.

rgely due to its climatic advantages as an AUTUMN AND WINTER HEALTH RESORT. The
e and clear sky. The establishment is heated throughout, and is most suitable for patients

For Prospectus of Terms, apply to J. W. GREW, Manager.

Deal. Wooden royal arms, suitably painted and gilded, above the entrance to the Royal Hotel

Below
Worthing. Warnes Hotel: a lively display of Regency detail where the only intrusion is by modern plumbing, disguised but not hidden by white paint

along the quay between the hotel and the harbour, so guests would constantly be reminded of the company's activities and would presumably have considered this to be an added attraction. The description quoted in the company's *Holiday Notes* booklet gives a good idea of what kind of customer the hotel was built for and what facilities such a place had to offer. After describing the views across the estuary and other attractions the hotel is described as follows: 'Here we found, during a recent visit, the appointments of a first class character. There is a very elegant coffee-room facing the harbour, conversation and reading rooms facing the piers, excellent billiard, bath, and smoking rooms, and some 50 good bedrooms. The cuisine and cellar are both of the best, and altogether more comfortable headquarters for a seaside holiday, or Friday to Monday "pick-me-up", . . . could hardly be desired.' It is not a description that would attract a modern parent looking for a family hotel, but this was the age in which children were seen but not heard, even at seaside hotels. The aim of the proprietors was to offer accommodation, of a standard a little above that which their customers might enjoy in their homes, for a mainly middle class clientele.

By this time families with their inconveniently conspicuous broods sought refuge in boarding houses. Hotels were for ladies and gentlemen and for those who wished to be regarded as such. It is hardly surprising that their appeal exploited snobbery and that a passion for grandeur dominated their architects' drawing boards. When successful north country mill owners were building incredible palaces for themselves on the fringes of Lancashire and Yorkshire towns, and the aristocracy were busy spreading fake castles over the English and Scottish landscape, the grand hotels offered a taste of the same ostentatious high living, if only for a fortnight during the holiday season. The largest of them managed to achieve an image of grandeur which even the most wealthy industrialist might envy and which could make a Hollywood film set seem credible by comparison. Two of them, both opened in the

Scarborough. The grandest of the Grand Hotels

Below
Scarborough. Grand Hotel: detail of the entrance

Left
Ilfracombe hotel. A heavy-handed gothic pile purpose-built in the 1860s as an hotel with 250 rooms

Below left
Worthing. Burlington Hotel: detail of the entrance

Right
Tenby. Early nineteenth century hotel facade overlooking the harbour

1860s, can be taken as examples of what all the others hoped to achieve. The Grand Hotel at Scarborough was built in 1867 at a cost of £100,000; the Grand at Brighton opened in 1864 at a cost of £150,000. The Great Eastern at Harwich is a doll's house by comparison.

Both of these hotels remain in use today and both retain something of their original atmosphere. To appreciate their true significance, however, they must be set against the background of mid-Victorian England with its extremes of wealth and poverty, its pride in British achievement and conviction of British superiority. Both hotels were opened in true Victorian style and the opening ceremonies and the wonders of each were fully reported at the time. The *Brighton Herald* of 23 July 1864 (also the year the Great Eastern at Harwich opened) rose to the occasion with a fine display of provincial journalism. It described the Grand as standing on 'our cliffs like Saul amidst the men of Israel'. Continuing in a similar vein: 'Its multitudinous windows with their gilded balconies, and the brackets which run up the centre of the building, and the cornices, and the top gilded finials are the most striking external features'. The central concourse was covered by 'a lustrous Dome which casts down its soft and subdued light upon you'. No expense appears to have been spared in the decorations or the more mundane services and appointments. There were walls decorated in the fashionable italianate style and conservatories lined with Minton tiles. The public rooms included smoking rooms, billiard rooms, a ladies' coffee room and a gentlemen's coffee room. The catering in such an establishment had to be entirely self-sufficient and the kitchens therefore extended to a bakehouse, fish and roasting departments, a confectionery, wine and beer cellars and even an icehouse. Cooking and lighting were by gas.

Visitors reached their bedrooms by five passenger lifts operated by means of the 'down pressure of a 60 foot column of water being so applied as to drive the ram which upheaves the

platform'. The displacement of air this caused was used to ventilate the building: the Victorians were shrewd in their economy, as well as inventive. The *Brighton Herald* further listed the materials used in the construction: 15 miles of wallpaper, 12 miles of bell wire, 230 marble chimney pieces and so on. The article concluded that 'in no other country in Europe could so beautiful a building with such appliances for the enjoyment of life have been erected, fitted up, furnished and stocked in the short period of 18 months'. The reporter nevertheless expressed his personal preference for the Bedford Hotel as 'decidedly the best specimen of hotel architecture in Brighton'.

The Grand Hotel at Scarborough opened on 25 July 1867 with a banquet and ball for 200 guests. It was the culmination of four years' work on the site. The architect, Cuthbert Broderick, was considered to be a master of the grandiose seldom equalled even among nineteenth century architects. His town hall at Leeds does more than any other building or group of buildings to give that city European status. At Scarborough Broderick met the challenge of a spectacular site on St Nicholas Cliff with an assurance which even today can arouse emotions either of hatred or admiration. The monstrous pile he created was composed of more than six million yellow bricks; it conceded nothing to the quiet dignity of the Regency terraces which until its arrival had given Scarborough its character as the pre-eminent northern spa.

After more than a century it continues to dominate, as the architect obviously intended it should. Its landward façade rises 112 feet above the road, crowned by an ornate roofline with beehive-shaped domes topped by viewing platforms. On the seaward side the building descends 160 feet from roof to base. What occurs between can be described as a monument to the Victorian concept of material comfort and good living. This was a hotel that had to rival and if possible surpass the standard of living which the wealthiest men in Europe experienced in their own homes. That it was successful was as much due to its architectural magnificence, inside and out, as to its standards of catering, service and social tone. An early rule required that 'ladies will not wear bonnets; gentlemen will wear black frock or dress coats' in the dining room. Hotels such as this have to meet social changes, usually by becoming conference centres catering for a year round trade, although the need to keep going for longer than the summer season was recognised from the start when the Grand advertised that 'during the winter months Haden's Warming Apparatus will be in operation, rendering the hotel a warm, dry and agreeable winter residence'.

The main entrance of the Grand Hotel expressed something of the opulence of the interior, with its lavish use of relief decoration and flamboyant disregard of stylistic purity. Scattered around the coastline are a number of hotels which were built in the Grand manner (the huge and isolated Headland Hotel at Newquay, designed by Sylvanus Trevail and opened in 1891, is an example) and these were the antecedents of the great metropolitan and international hotels associated with the Edwardian era. The smaller hotels may have imitated some of their mannerisms (for example, the doorway of the Burlington Hotel, Worthing, with its odd mixture of mermaids, arabesques, classical detail and a Neptune's head as keystone) but they were aimed at a different clientele.

Popular guidebooks of the latter part of the nineteenth century, particularly the immensely successful Black's and Murray's series, carried sections, usually on cheap coloured paper, devoted to advertisements for hotels, and these give interesting indications of the custom they were out to attract and of the services clients could expect. In the 1880s the Ilfracombe Hotel 'on the verge of the Atlantic' was advertising 'five acres of ornamental grounds; six Lawn-Tennis courts; 250 rooms' in addition to 'one of the largest Swimming Baths in England; also Private Hot and Cold Sea and Fresh Water Baths, Douche, Shower, &c'. The advertisement also stated, significantly, that

Ilfracombe. Early Victorian hotel landscape changed only by concrete lamp posts, television masts and the ubiquitous parking poles

'the means of communication with Ilfracombe by Railroad and Steamboat are most complete'. Road access is not mentioned.

Many hotels had direct communication, by means of covered ways, with station platforms and those which were not so favourably equipped had either porters in attendance or sent their own horsedrawn omnibus to meet trains. Apart from such ease of communication between the hotel and London or other great cities the possibilities for tours or walks in the neighbourhood were also considered to be of importance. Before the invention of the motor car it was often thought better to build your hotel at the local place of interest or natural beauty to enable visitors to explore it on foot or see it from the windows of the hotel. Many of these places remain comparatively wild and inaccessible. At least the motor car and caravan have the virtue that, being mobile, they go away. One such place with a permanent building was Lynton, where the Valley of Rocks Hotel, built in 1888, was 'situated in its own Magnificent Grounds 600 feet above and facing sea'.

These late Victorian hotels had all the architectural characteristics of their period and they set out to do for the professional and upper middle classes what the earlier, larger and more sumptuous establishments did for the wealthy and noble. The Ilfracombe Hotel is now the municipal offices and its ornate gothic features are patternbook examples of a form of architecture that was made to serve many diverse purposes. Built in 1868 it is in its way as typical of the period as the Grand Hotels already described. The groups of decorated lancet windows, the high pitched roof punctuated by rows of dormer windows and topped by iron crestings, and its heavy buttressed chimneys have parallels all over the country. The nearby Westward Ho! Hotel at Northam, and the Valley of Rocks Hotel have more restrained but still unmistakably Victorian gothic characteristics. This was a period when the public at large were enjoying the picturesque scenery revealed by poets and painters a century or more earlier; if their hotels contrived to resemble castles or medieval palaces so much

the better.

Things began to change when the motor car appeared on the roads at the turn of the century. Not only did these vehicles change the demands travellers made upon accommodation: they also caused a change in attitudes which has reached its climax in our own times. Hotels could no longer remain romantic retreats, cut off from the world except for a tenuous link by rail with the big cities. Some of the romance of inaccessible places would soon be gone for ever but it was replaced by a new excitement which was to produce a new type of holiday and a new type of hotel to meet its needs. The days when hotels could attract visitors merely by offering 'drawing rooms, lounge, smoking and billiard rooms, all facing the sea' were soon to be over. Such phrases as 'motor garage and petrol' began to appear in advertisements and prospectuses, often alongside 'posting and stabling'. Devon, Cornwall and the Lake District were the first regions to feel the full impact of the new freedom of movement, and to take a car up Porlock Hill was to prove that you were a real motorist not just a 'Sunday outer'. As the car was ousting the horse so the gothic pile and the cottage *ornée* were being replaced by the brash redbrick and terra-cotta of the Edwardian period. Both the good taste of the Regency and the romance of Victorian had given way to a new style; it was self-assertive, made little reference to the past, and paved the way to the uninhibited seaside architecture that was to come in the twenties and thirties.

The fashionable society of Edward VII's reign was essentially urban. For seaside holidays it rediscovered the French and Italian Rivieras and so transformed the Mediterranean coastline. The vast and grandiose hotels of this epoch are not in Scarborough or Brighton, but Nice, Cannes, Monte Carlo and Biarritz, though a few grandiose hotels were built at expanding resorts on the English south coast at the turn of the century. Folkestone provides some excellent examples.

Folkestone has for many years derived trade from its harbour,

Below
Boarding house lounge. A period piece from the thirties: note the wallpaper, carpet, fireplace, cane chairs and occasional table, light fitting and even the flower arrangements, all 'modern' and typical

Bottom
Hotel scene typical of the early 1930s. Redbrick and gabled building, white painted verandah and, of course, tennis

Typical 'hotel postcard' of the turn of the century. Note the oppressively heavy architecture in contrast to earlier gaiety

HYDRO HOTEL EASTBOURNE FROM THE SEA

Octagon House, 19 Derby Road, Douglas

Biarritz. Fading Edwardian splendours: a delightfully French response to the demands of the period

Biarritz. Edwardian confidence in luxury shown in the gateway to the Palace Hotel and the terrace of less grandiose hotels behind it

particularly in times when bad weather could hold up the Channel packets for days on end. In the 1850s the Pavilion Hotel advertised that 'refreshment of any kind can be had at a minute's notice (cold meat always ready) . . . so that parties passing on will receive immediate attention'. The development of the town as a family resort and as a place in which middle class private schools flourished came at about the same time. It was not however until the latter years of the century that major developments along the seafront began with the construction of hotels along the western end of The Leas. The Metropole originally stood in an isolated position, the domes and cupolas of its front facing out across the Channel and loftily overlooking the bandstand that was built in front of it a little later. The Metropole and the Grand (built in 1900) are among the last of the seaside hotels in the tradition that began nearly 40 years earlier. The rundown Royal Palace facing the harbour is a smaller but equally flamboyant example of the style which was effectively killed by the First World War.

Victorian monumentality progressed via Edwardian flamboyance to the 'madly gay' period between the wars, when the impact of the jazz age and the introduction of chromium plate, reinforced concrete and plate and coloured glass made less impression on hotel design than on cinemas, teashops and dance halls. Although connected with jazz and with 'flappers' the architectural style of the twenties had little to do with the negro culture from which the popular music of the period evolved. Although essentially superficial, having its finest achievements in decoration rather than architectural form, the jazz age proved highly inventive during its short existence. Its harshly mechanical, brashly exciting qualities are only now being recognised by architectural critics and historians. Osbert Lancaster was shrewd enough to describe it under the heading 'Modernistic' in his *Pillar to Post*, first published in 1938. Lancaster treats the period with witty abuse, a useful counter to the writings of contemporary authors who would have its style taken more seriously as 'Art

Scarborough. A mixture of architectural styles from Regency to rustic via the grandiose, all contributing to a highly individual and successful scene dominated by the Grand Hotel

Deco'. Its most important monuments in Britain included the Whitehall Cinema and the Strand Palace Hotel. Although the former is now demolished, the latter has its foyer preserved in the Victoria and Albert Museum. The wealthy and fashionable society of the time had little interest in traditional seaside holidays so nothing like the Strand Palace appeared on an astonished seafront in England.

The most significant change in the pattern of seaside holidays following the invention of the motor car has taken place since the last war. It may well be that we shall never again see the emergence of an architectural form peculiar to the needs of the hotel. It was a late Victorian phenomenon never to be repeated, yet curiously the number of people using hotels is increasing spectacularly each year; in certain areas the rush to supply the need is despoiling coastlines at a rate previously unknown. The essential difference between the older hotels and those of today lies in their purpose and the people for whom they cater. The nineteenth century hotelier looked towards the aristocrat, the wealthy and the upper middle class for his clientele; his buildings reflected this. Now the wealthy, though still making use of hotels, prefer to take their holidays in more exclusive surroundings and are prepared to travel the world to reach them. To provide nearer home for the limited season package holiday customer a new type of hotel has appeared. It must look modern, and to this end the examples built in the sixties had as many architectural gimmicks as the jazz age hotel had in its time. The aim now is not for grandeur or an atmosphere of opulence but for a uniformity of amenities, hygienic plumbing, comfort and well cooked food. Apart from the fact that as many bedrooms as possible must have balconies with views of the sea, in order to justify the claims of publicity brochures, the specific architectural demands are few. Today's holiday hotel must be built at minimum cost and yet be obviously (often aggressively) modern so as to impress the client that he is getting not only the best but the most recent in accommodation.

A typical resort development which is the direct result of the early success of package tour holidays is Jessollo, on the Adriatic coast at the eastern edge of the Venetian Lagoon. Until a few years ago it was no more than a village of the name a mile or so inland of a shoreline fringed with peach orchards. Now it is a strange mixture of seafront plots, some occupied by new hotels, others unused and covered by scrub or old shacks. The roads, laid out in a period of over-enthusiasm, can send four lanes of traffic heading straight into an undeveloped wilderness where the metalled surface ends in sand. A road along the landward side of the hotels is packed with souvenir stalls and shops, most of them crammed with coloured Venetian glass from Murano tortured into monstrous shapes. Where the hotels stop the camp and caravan sites start. The hotel buildings are concrete towers, displaying an impressive range of the decorative and often useless excrescences of contemporary achitecture. They are hotels in the tradition of fairground and exhibition architecture. Whatever they may be to the purist they are new and exciting to the holidaymaker and this is all they are intended to be. What will happen when the novelty wears off can only be guessed.

In the present decade a 'second generation' of mass market hotels is springing up along many miles of the Mediterranean coast, on mainlands and islands, and there are plans to develop large areas of previously untouched coastline between the Spanish frontier and the Carmargue. From among the sham and the superficial some genuine architectural forms are beginning to emerge, ranging from proposals for a hotel built into a sheer rockface on a Maltese cliff to pyramidal structures in an old French fishing port. These could be good omens, for hotel building has reached distinctive standards when it has sought to offer a larger than life background to living and to this end has used a slightly exaggerated version of the architecture of its period. Like exhibition design it can have the dual attraction of highlighting the contemporary while suggesting a possible future.

Seaton, Devon. A mock castle now successfully transformed into flatlets

Overleaf
The Albion Hotel, Broadstairs. An early example of a purpose-built seaside hotel, opened in 1816, which is still in use today. The exterior has hardly been altered

In this context present day developments could prove most interesting, provided that the rush to cater for the holiday explosion does not wipe out what character remains and does not overlook the singular opportunities suggested by seaside traditions, atmosphere, landscapes and marine activity.

The greatest potential dangers in the present situation are those of scale, both of individual buildings and of the complexes of which many form part. There are also the dangers inherent in any period of frenzied building activity, when standards of design and construction are likely to be sacrificed in the rush to put up more and more faster and faster. Neither problem is new nor is either confined to the seaside, but it is here that unsatisfactory solutions are more likely to have disastrous consequences than elsewhere if they are not recognised and satisfactorily dealt with.

The resorts which blossomed within a short period at the beginning of the last century on the southern coasts of England must have caused as great a disturbance to local populations as the mushrooming resorts of the Costa Brava do to Spanish fishermen of today. That they did not destroy the landscape was due to a variety of factors, the most important of which was the relatively small scale of each development. They were tiny oases of sophistication and urban life each in a wide rural hinterland. They also harmonised with surrounding nature and scenery, both from necessity and choice. Landscape design was still a subject of interest and a matter of practical achievement in England; a feeling for rightness, for balance between buildings and natural or contrived landscapes, dominated town and country. At a time when every cubic yard of soil to be moved had to be displaced by spade and wheelbarrow the temptation to flatten every site before starting to build was less overpowering than it appears to be today.

The upsurge of middle class prosperity in England between the wars caused a rash of bungalow and villa estates which virtually buried the entire southern coastline from the Thames estuary to the Solent, and the post-war years have seen the plugging of any gaps that had been left unfilled. Along this stretch of coastline the relationship between building and a once delightfully intimate landscape has been destroyed for ever by a combination of uniform banality of design and sheer weight of numbers. The only exceptions to the miserable rule are, paradoxically, the areas which had been developed in an earlier and more sympathetic period. Those countries whose sunshine attracts the mass tourist industry now face a similar problem, but on a vaster scale.

The most spectacular and in some respects most encouraging of the large scale developments along the Mediterranean is at Languedoc Rousillon, where the French southern coast begins to curve towards Spain. The size of this undertaking would have aroused the admiration of the railway builders of the last century, and the willingness of its sponsors to indulge in architectural experiments would also have met with their approbation. La Grande Motte, the centre of this enterprise, presents a landscape which is spectacularly different from the dreary lines of slab blocks which dwarf the bays and beaches not only around the Mediterranean but also throughout America. If we have to accept the fact that new resorts must continue to be built and that the coasts of the world are destined to be converted into massive holiday towns then La Grande Motte offers a more optimistic view of the future than Famagusta or most of the other booming areas. The package tour operators, with their disregard of anything but what their customers want for a fortnight each year, and their preparedness to ruin mile upon mile of previously unspoilt coast (and possibly the livelihood of local populations) in order to provide it, have a great deal to answer for.

The architects and designers of La Grande Motte, with its harbour, houses, clubs and ingenious pyramidal appartment blocks, have brought to the problem a spirit of adventure and excitement which is in the great tradition of holiday building. Elsewhere there are other indications that a new and worthy

Right
Hotel Do Mar, Sesimbra, Portugal. In striking contrast to Aldeia São Pedro (below), this hotel applies the principles of contemporary architecture to the design of seaside accommodation and the result is original and successful. Both of these recent Portuguese developments display the kind of architectural initiative and self-confidence which is in the best seaside tradition

Left
Biarritz. Aggressive 'modern', unrelated to site or function

Below left
Aldeia São Pedro, Portugal. A modern holiday village, mainly for foreign tourists, built in unashamed imitation of local vernacular architecture. Like much of the best seaside building it succeeds in spite of its defiance of accepted standards of architectural behaviour

approach to seaside architecture may be developing, but the visual squalor of most of the developments of the last two decades cannot be ignored. La Grande Motte is, for the present at least, for the comfortably well off but it is designed for mass use. What hope is there for the holidaymaker who wishes to spend his savings on a couple of weeks on the sun-drenched sands of the Mediterranean, or for the seeker after comparative solitude? For the former, tragically, there seems at present to be no alternative to the characterless tower block. For the latter there appears to be no hope at all.

Portmeirion, that whimsically nostalgic collection of italianate buildings and architectural follies built into the wooded slopes above the sands of Traeth Bach near Portmadoc in the years between the wars, re-stated the need to relate people to buildings and buildings to landscape in an intimate and highly personalised way. It is as far removed in concept from the tower block resorts as a wayside halt is from Paddington station, and yet it indicates an approach that is still feasible and lessons that still have to be learnt. Whimsy and nostalgia are essential ingredients of the best of seaside architecture, and relative scale is the first essential of any successful architectural or landscape composition. The architect of Portmeirion, Clough Williams-Ellis, may be catering exclusively for a wealthy clientele but this does not invalidate his work or make some of its achievements inapplicable to other or larger scale problems. After all, the Brighton Pavilion was the successful precedent for a vast amount of building for holidaymakers much lower down the social scale than the Prince Regent.

One particularly interesting attempt to provide modern amenities in a seaside hotel without destroying the scale of its situation is the Hotel Do Mar at Sesimbra in Portugal. The use of terracing and of simple geometric units repeated within an overall framework has kept the building in scale with its surroundings and retained an intimate character, particularly from within the

complex. It contrasts with another recent Portuguese development, the newly built and as yet uncompleted tourist village of Aldeia São Pedro in the Algarve. The Sesimbra hotel pattern could be repeated on a larger scale but it is difficult to see Aldeia São Pedro as anything more than an updated southern Portmeirion (except that most of the Portmeirion buildings are genuine antiques whereas those at the Portuguese village are modern within an imitation vernacular cladding which is unexpectedly successful). The rules of architectural good taste never seem to apply at the seaside.

La Grande Motte. This large scale urban development in the south of France is the contemporary equivalent of the Regency resorts. It is imposed upon the landscape with little regard for pre-existing standards or uses. Its architects have thus had the opportunity to experiment with new forms on a scale and in a manner normally available only to exhibition designers. Whether the result is a happy combination of architects dream and holidaymakers' paradise remains to be seen.

Chapter 5

CAMPS AND CHALETS

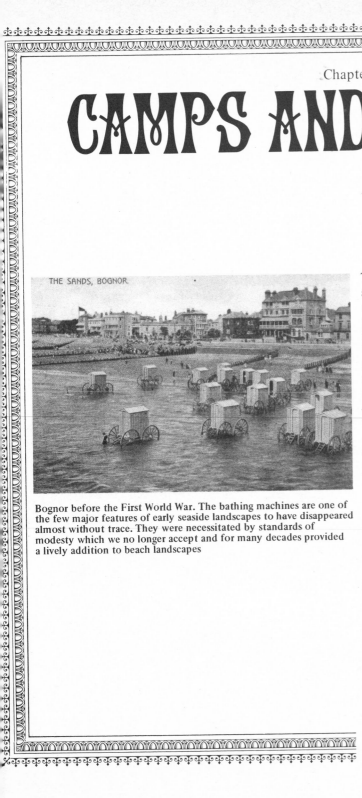

THE SANDS, BOGNOR.

Bognor before the First World War. The bathing machines are one of the few major features of early seaside landscapes to have disappeared almost without trace. They were necessitated by standards of modesty which we no longer accept and for many decades provided a lively addition to beach landscapes

The beach huts that are now a familiar sight at any English resort are the direct descendants of the bathing huts whose existence spanned well over a century from Regency times to the inter-war years. Bathing huts, or more properly 'machines', are one of the few features of the Victorian seaside that have failed to survive. Their passing has removed something of the essential character from the English holiday beach. They were an odd mixture of the elegant and clumsy, the functional and absurd. Their under-carriages had something of the delicacy of a passenger coach, enhanced by the ground clearance of the floor of the hut itself, which was necessary to enable it to be drawn into a sufficient depth of water to allow for complete immersion when the bather exited into the sea. The actual hut, sufficiently large to allow crinolined dresses to be peeled off and replaced by almost equally voluminous bathing dresses, usually had a platform at the back (or landward end) from which the machine was entered through a door; another door at the front led on to steps. The earliest machines were little more than rather cumbersome changing rooms and served convenience rather than modesty. The Victorian passion for making the slightest glimpse of human flesh a sin produced a variety of forms for the front end of bathing machines, designed to allow the bather to enter the water without the embarrasment of being observed.

This is hardly surprising, as early nineteenth century cartoons indicate that bather-watching (with or without the aid of telescopes) was a favourite sport, particularly enjoyed in an age which still awaited the invention of the bathing costume and which perforce found nudity the only practical alternative. The invention of the bathing machine is variously attributed, but the inventor of its extension, the 'modesty hood', is known to be a Margate Quaker named Beale. In the course of time the modesty hood took various forms, from a collapsible canvas tunnel completely covering the passage from hut to water, to an angled extension of the side walls which gave the machine a mid-

Tenby is a resort which, apart from having no pier, possesses practically everything that the Victorians required. Its attractions include excellent sands and spectacular cliffs; impressive antiquities and picturesque streets; a harbour; plenty of places worth visiting on boat trips, including nearby Caldy Island; fine coastal walks; and accessibility from London along the prestige route of the Great Western Railway. Even now its groups of clifftop hotels remain possibly the finest composite examples of nineteenth century seaside building and it has remained remarkably free from such twentieth century intrusions as amusement arcades. It is, perhaps, significant that it is immensely popular

twentieth century look. A small window was placed high up in the side of the box, for ventilation only, and bargeboards with or without pierced decoration completed the picture. A combination of less prudish attitudes and increasing crowds on the beaches brought about the final demise of the bathing machine sometime between the wars. By this time, however, it had already been replaced by the static hut, which took up less room on the beach but which lacked a great deal in character.

A natural successor to the mobile bathing hut was the tent, still commonly seen on continental beaches but virtually extinct in England. The gay colours of their striped canvas, together with those of the multi-coloured sunshades which are also a feature of European beaches, now have a particularly continental flavour, but until the outbreak of the Second World War they were still common around the coasts of England. It is difficult to explain why these gay little cubicles should have disappeared from the English scene; their lack of durability may have something to do with it. Most resorts derive a steady income from the letting of wooden huts, usually placed adjacent to the beach and serving the needs of families taking bed, breakfast and evening meal at a local boarding house. The English climate demands greater protection for holidaymaking families than can be offered by a beach tent, and wooden huts can in any case just as easily be removed in the off season for maintenance and repair. In some places the wooden huts are to be found in limited communities of dozens or less; elsewhere they almost constitute small townships and it is surprising how even such uniform structures can become individually interesting by the application of paint, the addition of names such as 'Isners', 'Happy Days' or 'Werere'. At Walton-on-the-Naze a colony of huts south of the pier demonstrates how easily uniformity can be transformed into variety.

The huts have to be of a more or less standard pattern in order to conform to a tight layout, but the variations on a limited theme are fascinating. Boarding is either vertical or horizontal,

A nostalgic view of Eastbourne. Apart from the clothes and the bathing machines little has changed so far as the ingredients of the seaside holiday are concerned

THE BEACH, EASTBOURNE

Below
Bathing tents. These were once a feature of British as well as Continental beaches. Although still very much in evidence across the Channel they have almost disappeared from British resorts

MIXED BATHING, FOLKESTONE

lapped or tongued and grooved. Gable ends are decorated or unadorned, infilled with trellis, panelling or slatted woodwork or left open. The tiny porticoes have rails or boarded panels; windows are curtained or shuttered. The whole effect, enhanced by a range of colours like a paintmaker's chart, is an informal, gay and happy compromise between privacy and community.

Properly sited these huts pose few problems so far as the landscape is concerned. They are part of the holiday scene to which few can object. The random collections of shacks, upturned boats, converted railway coaches (still found in some places) and the like are a different matter. Readers of Dickens will be aware that structures of this kind are nothing new, but often large areas of shacks and chalets, used both for holidays and as permanent residences, are a comparatively recent phenomenon. They are not necessarily ugly or offensive; some examples have an eccentric charm which makes an important contribution to seaside architecture. The verandahed huts, painted black and white and individually set into the base of the cliffs at Branscombe, between Seaton and Sidmouth, are delightfully lighthearted and yet do not detract from the remoteness or grandeur of the landscape. The same can be said of similar groups along the Cumberland coast and elsewhere. The key to their success lies in their scale and in their relationship with the forms of a landscape which remains dominant. Where the huts and chalets overrun the landscape they become a serious problem.

The worst example of shack development is probably at Jaywick, near Clacton-on-Sea, where acre upon acre of bungalows, huts and shacks completely obliterate the existing landscape without any awareness of the need to consider overall planning or design. Linked to the nearby sprawl of more or less permanent caravans at St Osyth's beach the result is monotony at best and squalor at worst, and yet to many thousands of people it must represent the seaside.

The distinction of being the first bungalow town is thought to belong to Shoreham-by-Sea where the spit of land running between the River Adur and the sea was first used as a site for converted railway carriages in 1890. They probably had a great deal more character then than the dreary suburbia with which the site is now covered. The fishermen's huts and holiday dwellings on the windswept shingle wastes of Dungeness prove that character is of greater importance than mere architectural distinction in creating a environment worth inhabiting. Some of the shacks on Dungeness are made from old railway carriages, others are built from timber or asbestos put together in a variety of ingenious ways. Boats, tackle, a magnificent modern lighthouse and its predecessor, even a concrete observation tower (a wartime relic) rising from a group of huts, together create an intriguing and unique seaside landscape which even the immense bulk of the nearby nuclear power station has failed to destroy. Until now the shingle has protected Dungeness from the inroads of the speculative builder, but the suburban villas are creeping out from Littlestone-on-Sea and Greatstone. They, with their plastic gnomes on lawns laid on imported soil, are destroying the character of this strangely beautiful but naturally inhospitable region.

The difference between the old huts and the new semi-detached houses is twofold. The huts are mainly inhabited by boatmen and fishermen whose intuitive response to sea and landscape is seen in their collections of boats and tackle, in the use of pitch and tar, and in the generally workaday atmosphere of their buildings. The inhabitants of the suburban villas have little or no connection with the sea or with the intensely 'local' landscape of shingle and characteristic flora on which their dwellings have been built. The apparent impermanence of the fishermen's huts is an unwitting acknowledgment of the dominance of the sea and the wind. In the same situation the brick semis and their neat suburban gardens are smugly out of place. It is all a question of the right response to a particular place.

Walton-on-the-Naze. A delightful collection of beach huts. One basic form, many shapes and an infinite variety of colours, particularly when the scene is animated by occupants

Old railway carriages can be either an eyesore or a delight. The group of old Great Western carriages used as camping coaches in the sidings at Dawlish Warren are perfectly in keeping with their situation as well as being a subtle memorial to the past glories of that splendid railway. The same coaches dumped willy-nilly on the beach would have a totally different effect. On the beach they would all too easily decay into an inappropriate and squalid mess. At the station they remain part of the railway, and as such their very impermanence, their hint of mobility, is part of their essential character and attraction.

A similar situation arises from the use of the much maligned caravan as a holiday home. The damage done to the landscape by many caravan camps is undeniable but the fault lies not so much in the caravan as in the design and layout of the sites they occupy. The design of caravans has, in fact, reached a high level, far ahead of that of many buildings. The first caravans intended for towing behind cars were built just after the First World War from army surplus materials. Their form was influenced as much by aircraft design (lightweight constructions of canvas and wooden struts) as by that of the horse-drawn caravan. From these origins the modern touring caravan has been designed to give a maximum of convenient and usable space within minimum volume and weight. Mobility has always been a first consideration, and so successful were the early designs that touring caravans have changed little in essentials for more than 30 years. Only during the last few years, with the introduction of mass-produced lightweight plastic mouldings and improvements in the design of fittings has a new approach to caravan design become possible. Far from being a menace the mobile caravan along with the frame tent has provided one of the few acceptable answers to the mid-twentieth century problem of vast numbers of people demanding seaside accommodation for three or four months of the year. To satisfy this demand by using permanent structures would have meant the total obliteration of most of the coastline of Europe within a very short period.

Royan. Typical European beach 'architecture'

Below
Branscombe, Devon. One more chalet could destroy the delicate balance but this little group with their bright paint and obvious impermanence snuggle neatly into the protective hillocks and are wholly appropriate

Dungeness. Wartime relics and impermanent hutments on a bare shingle
plateau exposed to the sea winds. A landscape full of character, retaining
something of the pioneer spirit of the outback in an overcrowded island

An early caravan, 1930. The adapted rear half of a Yorkshire bus, towed by a 12 hp Austin Burnham saloon

What has not yet been achieved is an application of the example of the tent and mobile caravan to the needs of static holiday accommodation, although several interesting experiments have been made. One of the most important of these was a mobile shelter designed and built several years ago by a group of art students. This consisted of a folding box built on to a caravan chassis. The sides of the box hinged in such a way that on site they could be used as extensions to the central unit and thus form a series of rooms with walls of PVC-coated nylon sheeting. Everything needed for a holiday home was contained within the unit, which could be towed wherever it might be required. Although not as mobile as the touring caravan the mobile shelter suggested many answers to some of the basic problems of temporary accommodation, including the desirability of an original and exciting environment at holiday times. The protype was towed by Land Rover from London to Milan for exhibition, thus demonstrating its practicality. Its advantages lie in its all-weather protection combined with ease of movement and storage. The conventional static caravan lacks both of these qualities, although it remains nominally a mobile object.

Unfortunately, the word caravan has become associated in many people's minds with the static rather than the touring kind, and this has led to a strange inability on the part of many architects and planners to recognise the immense contribution that truly mobile units could make to solving the increasing problems of the provision of holiday accommodation. The principles involved are so misunderstood that an eminent architect and designer, writing on the subject recently, suggested that they should be painted to merge with their surroundings in order to lessen their impact on the landscape. No one would suggest that permanent buildings should be camouflaged in this way: rather that they should be imaginatively designed and properly sited. The advantage of the mobile unit is that it carries all necessary services with it, and thus demands nothing more from the landscape than

This Caravan Club site won a Civic Trust award, the first site to achieve such distinction, for its screening and landscaping work. It is situated in East Lothian, Scotland

Below
Beacon Park, St Agnes, Cornwall. A Caravan Club site for touring caravans, excellently screened and yet making the most of its superb situation

The beginnings of bungalow development at Saltcoats. Like caravans, bungalows and chalets have been almost universally condemned by writers on landscape and architecture. Although much of this abuse has been justified they are not entirely without merit, as these examples show, and those built earlier in the century often display an awareness of locality and of the seaside tradition which is absent in most post-war estate development in Britain

Porthcawl, 1920. These rather featureless brick boxes are indicative of what was to follow, as bungalow estates rapidly engulfed great areas along the British coastline. They hardly differ either in concept or detail from much of what is being built more than half a century later

Below
Uncontrolled inter-war building

Bottom
Youth camps have been a regular summer feature of the British seaside since Baden-Powell first took the scouts to Brownsea Island in July 1907. This early scout camp was photographed at Bexhill in 1911 or 1912

ater supply. The whole concept of mobility is peculiarly English, indeed *le camping* was an English invention. On sites on the continent and in America the tendency to extend the built-in facilities of the caravan to a permanent provision of restaurants, toilet blocks, launderettes, entertainment halls, shops and so on has been less successfully resisted. This is a very different concept and poses a number of problems, as can be seen almost anywhere on the Adriatic coast of Italy or on the 'caravan coast' of Lincolnshire.

Where permanent facilities are provided on caravan sites there is a natural tendency to obtain the greatest financial return from them by encouraging long term or semi-permanent bookings and thus excluding the genuine touring customer. These sites then acquire some of the characteristics of permanent structures, a role for which the caravan was never designed. An encouraging development has been the entry of some of the older-established caravan manufacturers into the field of portable rather than mobile constructions, and it is here that the role of the mobile shelter may eventually come to be recognised. There is no reason why a well designed group of such shelters, properly integrated with the landscape, should be any less attractive than many of the traditional forms of seaside building. They are certainly more acceptable than the purpose-built holiday camps which have become a feature of the English coastline since the 1930s.

The complete failure of the major holiday camps to achieve even a semblance of the seaside holiday mood is one of the major environmental failures of the century.

This has in part arisen from a mistaken belief that the clientele they seek are unconcerned by such considerations (a visit to a good fairground should dispel such illusions) but more so perhaps because the camps are essentially inward looking. The seaside setting is important only in initial publicity. Everything the holidaymaker wants is usually provided within the camp itself and there is no pressing need to come to terms with the seaside environment. A holiday camp at Clacton-on-Sea is actually shut off from the seafront by a tall iron rail pallisade surmounted by barbed wire, and the view of the camp from the promenade could easily be mistaken for a film set for a prisoner of war epic. Occasionally there is a half hearted attempt to make abysmally dull buildings appear as suitable holiday setting, by the addition of coloured plastic panels, or even by the construction of a mock continental bistro complete with plastic grapevines. But almost without exception the English holiday camp is a failure in terms both of architecture and landscape.

This is particularly tragic in an age when advances in public entertainment have been so great and when there have been so many exciting exhibitions using just the kind of adventurous structures that would serve the needs of holiday camps so well. In most cases attempts at creating a holiday atmosphere by appropriate design treatment have been confined to interiors, but even here there has been nothing to match the Victorian Grand Hotel or the imaginative creations of the Blackpool Pleasure Beach.

In striking contrast to the typical English holiday camp the camps of the Club Méditerranée reveal a liveliness of approach that is wholly appropriate and in most cases highly successful. Aided by a kinder climate and longer season than England's, these camps have achieved a happy balance between the permanent and the temporary (many of the constructions are dismantled and stored for the winter) and they have also been able to provide new and exciting landscapes by subtle responses to existing features. The village at Arhziv, in Israel, is a particularly fine example. Based on hexagonal panels, each part of the village has a visual unity with the whole. The beach shelters or 'parasols' are made from linked hexagons. The material is compacted straw reinforced with wire; it has an attractive texture entirely in keeping with a sandy beach. The hexagon dominates both plan and elevations of the living accommodation as well as other parts of the camp. Textural variety is achieved by the use of stretched canvas for the covering of the sickbay panels, and by the intrusion of the natural

rock and vegetation into many views within the camp. The outdoor life concept of the Club Méditerranée may not suit all climates or all tastes, but its approach to planning is an object lesson which should be studied by all concerned with building at the seaside.

Essential to all seaside holiday provision is a clear understanding of its essentially impermanent nature (as expressed in the touring caravan), a sympathetic response to natural landscape and local design vernacular (a good example is the Talisman Island holiday community near New York) and a willingness to enter into the spirit of enjoyment which is the first essential for any holiday. The future of most of the world's coastlines may well depend on the speed with which these conditions are recognised and the skill with which they are met.

In England the changing pattern of holidaymaking is reflected in the increasing popularity of the touring holiday and of self-help accommodation. The English coast has been mercifully spared the blight of massive hotels packed side by side on minimal plots that is so common elsewhere. There are various reasons for this, the high costs of land, building and staff being among the most important. It would be comforting but inaccurate to imagine that it could not happen here, though planning control is stricter than in many European countries. The temptation to reap additional rate income could exercise considerable influence on many local authorities. Fortunately for us, the demand for massive hotel blocks hardly exists, and the needs of family holidaymakers are being increasingly met by camp and caravan sites, holiday flats, and bed and breakfast lodgings. The clue to the solution of future problems lies in impermanent and mobile structures. We have never been more able or willing to think in these terms.

Many Victorian and Edwardian hotels have become monumental white elephants, totally unsuited to modern conditions and frequently dominating a still-outraged landscape. Even holiday flats, however well designed, are destined to remain empty for the greater part of each year and empty properties are always a depressing feature, as well as representing low returns on invested capital. The authorities of the Pembroke National Park have set an important precedent in requiring all caravan sites to be virtually clear of caravans for the winter months. This requirement, coupled with a sympathetic attitude towards the establishment of new sites, succeeds in combining maximum holiday use with minimum landscape interference. That camp and caravan sites can actually improve a landscape is demonstrated by some of the awards the Caravan Club has received for its development of inland sites. The opportunity has yet to be provided for similar coastal developments; the pressures of commerce have so far excluded the non profit making clubs.

On farms and fields throughout the country the superbly designed and often brightly coloured caravans come and go throughout the short holiday season, enlivening the scene and leaving not a mark on the landscape. In extreme cases they offer a chance of survival to marginally profitable small farms and thus help to preserve rather than destroy the pattern of farming and vernacular farm buildings. In England the Caravan Club alone has nearly 100,000 members who with their families represent at least 300,000 people. That these can be absorbed into the summer landscape is a remarkable achievement, when one considers the damage the equivalent amount of permanent accommodation could cause.

The seasonal squalor of some English and continental campsites is no more an argument against camping as such than the decay of some buildings is an argument against architecture. The best of the holiday sites in England and abroad have achieved a standard in building and layout far better than anything to be seen in holiday camps or in most estate developments.

Early in the century the seaside villas of the fairly well to do began to spread outwards from the established resorts and into some of the smaller coastal towns or otherwise untouched

The 'Club Mediterranée Village' at Arviz. The use of octagonal screens in varied combinations is a lively solution to the problem of semi-permanent accommodation in a hot climate

Royan. Seafront villa, French style

Hayling Island. The infilling of the coastline without regard for either landscape or architecture

countryside. In England, houses that were often quaintly referred to as cottages, exhibiting remote influences of Voysey and architects of his period and looking like pen-drawn illustrations from *Studio* magazine, found their way into odd wooded corners of Devon or Somerset and other suitably picturesque locations. Between the wars the fashion was less for the pseudo-vernacular and more for the brash and obviously 'new'. Seaside villas were no longer the prerogative of the monied few; they were reaching down the social scale and multiplying. During this period many miles of English coastline became covered with villas, most of them in exaggerated styles ranging from pseudo-Corbusier to Dutch Colonial. For the first time in history popular art found popular expression in mass middle class housing.

The period was brief but frenzied, for the post-war years have witnessed an acceleration of quantity and an almost total disappearance of individuality as estate after estate of monotonously uniform and banal housing drearily cover more and more acres of coastal land. The Englishman's dream of retirement by the sea has been fulfilled, but too often, regrettably, in the sort of house identical to the one he left inland, only twice as costly.

The seashore villa in its heyday of the twenties was, in terms of seaside tradition and architecture, a parody of styles. If they were foreign, all the better. Timber structures reminiscent of Swiss chalets appeared (often before the access roads did) on the Essex coast, where they contrived to look very English. Every creek, inlet, beach or cliff along miles of coast seemed to acquire some quantity of villas or chalets ranging from double-fronted imitation half-timbered buildings complete with artificially rusted iron hinges on artificially studded oak doors to simple wooden huts rather like cricket pavilions. The latter were often charming individually, and were if suitably placed an attractive addition to the scene. Local variants, usually of a slightly more grandiose variety, appeared on the more accessible parts of the European

coastline. They are now accepted as part of the scene, and the early English examples provide some fascinating specimens of native eccentricity.

Chapter 6

TRANSPORT

LLANDUDNO.

EVAN JONES,

PRESCOT HOUSE, LLANDUDNO,

Has pleasure in announcing that on Monday, the 2nd of June, 1884, and upon every week day until September 27th, the magnificent FOUR-HORSE COACH,

"The   of
Prince   Wales.''

Will make a DAILY TRIP, starting from the Queen's Hotel, Llandudno, at eight o'clock each morning, and will, at a grand speed, do the distance from Llandudno, through Conway, along the picturesque slopes of the Carnarvonshire Hills, through Trefriw, Llanrwst, Bettws-y-Coed, Capel Curig, returning homewards through the renowned Pass of Nant Frangon, by Lord Penrhyn's leviathan Slate Quarries, Bethesda, past Penrhyn Castle, Llanfairfechan, Penmaenmawr, Conway, arriving at Llandudno at about half-past Seven o'clock the same Evening.

PASSENGERS' FARES :—For the Round, Twelve Shillings.

INTERMEDIATE DISTANCES PRO RATA.

Passengers are booked at PRESCOT HOUSE, MOSTYN STREET.

Leaves Queen's Hotel, Llan- dudno... ... 8.0 a.m.	Leaves Tanybwlch, Capel Curig Hotel ... 2.20 p.m.
,, Llandudno Junction Hotel ... ... 8.40 ,,	,, Royal Hotel do. 2.30 ,,
,, Conway (near the Old Castle) ... ... 8.45 ,,	Arrive at Penrhyn Slate Quarries and Bethesda ... 3.30 ,,
,, Llanbedr, Bedol Inn 9.45 ,,	Leaves Bethesda, Douglas
,, Trefriw, Belle Vue Hotel ... ... 10.20 ,,	Arms Hotel... 4.30 ,,
,, Llanrwst, Victoria Hotel... ... 10.40 ,,	,, Llanfairfechan, Castle Hotel 6.0 ,,
Arrive at Bettws-y-Coed, Gwydr Hotel 11.30 ,,	,, Penmaenmawr ... 6.20 ,,
Leaves Bettws-y-Coed .. 1.15 p.m.	,, Conway ... ... 7.0 ,, Arriving at Llandudno about... ... 7.30 ,,

The distance of the whole route, 56 Miles.

EVERY DAY (Sundays excepted and weather permitting) the large Brake "ENTERPRISE" will leave the Queen's Hotel, Llandudno, for a trip round to Colwyn Bay, through the Vale of Mochdre and back, *via* Llandudno Junction. starting at 10.30 a.m. and 2.50 p.m.

FARE 2s. 6d. EACH.

ALSO, a large Brake will leave the above-named Hotel for a trip through Conway, over the old coach road through the Sychnant Pass and down Dwygyfylchi and Penmaenmawr, and back along the new road, staying at Dwygyfylchi for half-an-hour, in order to allow passengers to view the Fairy Glen, and also half-an-hour at Penmaenmawr, starting at 9.30 a.m. and 3 p.m.

Fare for the Round, 4s. each.

As already mentioned, the development of the seaside as a holiday playground was controlled and conditioned by the expansion of the railways in the last century and by the motor car in this. Since the Second World War aircraft have opened up the world in the way that the railways did a century and a half previously, and increasing leisure among the affluent nations, combined with the packaged tour and the charter flight, have enabled millions of Europeans and Americans to explore new playgrounds and enjoy new sights and scenes. For the Victorians travel itself was a thrill; it became a pleasurable experience almost for the first time in history. Turner's portrait of a Great Western broad gauge locomotive at full speed, in his painting *Rain, Steam, and Speed*, symbolises the excitement steam travel added to life in the nineteenth century. It was a true Victorian, Robert Louis Stevenson, who wrote 'to travel hopefully is a better thing than to arrive'. Stevenson was a genuine traveller and experienced the wonder of exploration during that all too short period when it was possible for the adventurous to set foot on new ground without facing the extreme hazards of the traveller into the totally unknown.

As men land on the moon and London trippers swelter in traffic jams on the Colchester bypass on hot summer Saturdays it is difficult to acknowledge that travel from London to the seaside was until recently an experience to be looked forward to, enjoyed and re-lived. Rail travel caught the imagination of our ancestors, and the railway companies were not slow in exploiting its intrinsic appeal. They spent vast sums on the building of speculative lines into coastal wildernesses in the hope (frequently realised) that the railway would bring growth and prosperity. They engaged fashionable architects to design impressive edifices for their station buildings and some of them bought the land around their newly-opened lines in order to obtain maximum profit from the inevitable rise in land values once a service was established. The North Eastern Railway, for example, employed Cuthbert Broderick as

Cromer before the railway arrived

Cromer in 1905. A postcard view which conveys both the detail and the atmosphere of the scene and which also shows the excellence of many of the photographs used for the early postcards

Cromer from the Doctor's Steps

A coach tour in pre-charabanc days, 1907

architect for some of the stations on their lines to the Yorkshire coast; other equally eminent men were employed elsewhere.

The smoking, steaming monsters which hauled the trains survive only in old photographs but the monumental stations remain at many coastal resorts, some long severed from the lines which served them. The neglect of many of these fine buildings is surprising at a time when nostalgia for steam railways is a passion that grips millions. Not only the stations but also the engineering works along the lines deserve more widespread recognition and better treatment than some have received. Where the lines actually ran along the edge of the sea, as on the Furness Railway Company's route from Barrow to Whitehaven, the scenery itself was enough to command admiration. The old North Eastern line from Whitby to Stockton-on-Tees provided a spectacular ride between the wild moorlands and the immense cliffs between Whitby and Staithes, passing over superb viaducts at Sandsend on its way to the northerly resorts of Saltburn, Marske and Redcar. South of Whitby, *en route* for Scarborough, passengers were treated to magnificent views of Robin Hood's Bay as the trains struggled up the bank to Ravenscar. Ravenscar was laid out as a resort but the venture failed; today only a hotel, a few houses and shops, little-used roads and a derelict railway station survive on its windswept height.

The railways were quick to exploit their coastal lines and to advertise their attractions. Cheap excursions, season tickets and special holiday rates were all used to attract custom. Shortly after the introduction of the first Bank Holiday in 1871 day excursions were a regular and popular feature, and the Midland Railway advertised third class travel at a penny a mile in 1872. The competition to attract the crowds had begun and by 1885 the Great Eastern were advertising:

'FRIDAY OR SATURDAY TO TUESDAY AT THE SEASIDE. Every Friday and Saturday 1st, 2nd and 3rd class return tickets at reduced fares are issued as under by

Horse and dog transport awaiting custom at Brighton, 1905

Below
A holiday outing, Devon, 1926

A sea trip at Ramsgate, c.1900

Boats on the beach at Deal, c.1900

Sail and steam at Margate

Steamer at Birnbeck Pier, Weston-super-Mare

9 WESTON-SUPER-MARE. — The Old Pier. — LL.

E. S. ~ 161. BOU

all trains, available for return by any of the advertised trains on any day up to and including the Tuesday following the date of issue.'

The stations served were Hunstanton, Lowestoft, Yarmouth, Cromer, Walton-on-the-Naze, Clacton-on-Sea, Harwich, Dovercourt, Felixstowe, Aldeburgh and Southwold. It is interesting to note that among these towns Dovercourt was one of the earliest of east coast resorts; Clacton and Cromer developed late, following the arrival of the railway (Clacton being on a branch), and Aldeburgh and Southwold retain their character as older fishing and working towns to this day. Cromer in particular was a quiet little place near the sea, overwhelmed by massive Edwardian hotels along the front and transformed by the provision of holiday amenities in the last decades of the nineteenth century.

Probably the most successful exploitation of a scenically inspiring section of railway was that by the Great Western of the Devon coast between Dawlish and Brixham. Here the world-famed Cornish Riviera and Torbay Expresses ran. During the 1930s artists of the great period of railway poster design made full use of the scenery, the features of the line and the romance of travel. The evocative train names remain classics of their kind, along with the European 'Blue Trains' and the Orient Express, as symbols of the climax of the steam age. The quality and scale of the old Great Western, with its tunnels and beach-side track (often shown with waves breaking over the retaining wall and trains enveloped in sea spray), and the fine decorative ironwork and 'GWR' ciphers, are a tribute both to the skill and optimism of the railway promoters and engineers.

The influence of the railways from the mid-nineteenth to mid-twentieth century can be judged in some measure by the fact that Murray's Guides (probably the best guidebooks ever published) based their descriptions on journeys along the lines and from the various stations, on the assumption that users of the guides would naturally be travelling by train. Most of the railway

A steamer departing from the Clarence Pier, Southsea. Such scenes of activity and excitement were typical of the years up to the outbreak of the Second World War. They are probably the most significant feature of seaside holidays to have been made virtually extinct by the war

Below
A cross-Channel excursion boat entering Boulogne, c.1912

The Lynton and Lynmouth Railway. Probably the most spectacular cliff railway in Britain and almost certainly the best value for money to be obtained on public transport. Our ancestors were proud of their engineering skills and knew how to exploit them to the full. Travel was regarded as a potentially exciting experience; an end in itself as well as a means of reaching somewhere. The fact that many of their cliff railways still attract crowds and operate at a profit indicates how well they understood human nature

companies either owned or had an interest in the other forms of transport which met the traveller at his destination. Hotels in places served by the railways met the trains with their own horse-drawn and, later, motorised conveyances, and the railways frequently ran in conjunction with similar services to more remote places. For very many years the railways had competed with horse-drawn transport but now the horse was necessary to convey holidaymakers from the station to the hotel of their choice. The motor coach, or charabanc, opened up the prospect of scenic tours, with day or afternoon outings and mystery trips to more distant places. The Great Western, never willing to leave off at the end of the line, ran fleets of coaches in Wales and elsewhere and advertised trips by the company's buses as part of the holiday attractions of the resorts they served.

After the First World War these outings must have offered the first experience of motor travel to a whole generation for whom possession of a car was an unrealisable dream. Hard-tyred and open-topped they carried gay and wide-eyed crowds across the wastes of Exmoor or Dartmoor, into the Welsh mountains or Cumbrian lakes and fells, or merely along the uncluttered roads to the next resort.

Horse coaches had preceded the motor bus, and the earliest bus drivers dressed in the jodhpurs and leather leggings more appropriate to horse riding. Horse transport survived remarkably into the railway and motor age and as late as 1895 Jones Brothers of Lynton were advertising their 'well-appointed fast four-horse coach *Tantivy* (carrying the mails)' which ran 'daily throughout the year (Sundays excepted) in connection with the trains of L & SW Railway'. The horse has never lost its attraction and even now a few of the old open carriages remain at some resorts.

For the majority however the motor has taken over. Pride of the twenties was the open charabanc with its transverse rows of hard wooden bench seats, each row reached by its own door in the side of the vehicle. For inclement weather an enormous canvas

The new lighthouse, Portland Bill. An entirely appropriate seaside landscape. Shacks, sheds and shanties which would be unacceptable elsewhere seem somehow necessary to the total composition. The lighthouse and landmark give scale and purpose, the hutments introduce a necessary element of impermanence. Compare this with a south coast bungalow estate and the lessons to be learnt become obvious

Margate pier and harbour from a souvenir plate. Such prints, reminiscent of the works of Eric Ravilious and Edward Bawden, were produced in thousands for the decoration of souvenirs at the turn of the century

Scarborough lighthouse ('built by public subscription') from a tiny souvenir dish, as delightful as it is useless

Glass paperweights with pictures on the base were very popular as cheap souvenirs in the last century. This one shows an early view of Blackpool

Felixstowe ferry. A Martello tower and the remains of sea defences create a landscape of immense character

Aberayron, Cardiganshire. A coastal village and harbour in the vernacular tradition, showing the importance of colour on buildings

Scarborough cliff lift

BEACH CAFE

LIFT TO EAST HILL
GLORIOUS VIEWS AND WALKS

Hastings East Hill lift

hood was pulled over the entire coach and secured by leather straps to anchorages forward of the bonnet. These vehicles, high off the ground to give maximum viewing advantage and to minimise the effects of bumps, were entered by high step-like running boards (a difficult feat for the elderly).

A variant of the open coach, known familiarly as the 'toast rack', was designed to give even better viewing; it also incidentally exposed its passengers to additional hazards from wind and flying insects. These coaches had successive rows of seats stepped like those in a lecture theatre to give each row of passengers a view over the heads of those in front of them. Before the days of parking restrictions, rows of coaches and charabancs were parked along the seafronts and at other vantage points in the resorts. One attractive feature of those days which can still be seen occasionally is the collection of boards advertising various outings. Painted by the local signwriter, they usually showed destinations, times and prices in decorative lettering and were headed by naïve paintings of beauty spots and similar attractions *en route*. Such boards enlivened a number of east coast resorts until the Eastern National bus company was nationalised when, in the true spirit of bureaucracy, such evidences of individuality were disposed of. The tradition was of course inherited from the 'trips round the bay' and similar signs of the boatmen. One of the earliest coach tour operators had a board offering 'motor trips into the heart of Devon by the Lucky Horseshoe', unmistakably indicating their antecedents. The board showed a painted map of Devon at the centre of which was a large heart with a coach driving straight into it.

Boat trips have been popular since the earliest days of seaside holidays, and the characteristic landscape of heavy-sailed fishing boats pulled on to a sloping beach is one of the losses we have suffered in this century. They have been replaced by the clustered masts and sails of private dinghies. The visual impact of sturdy vernacular boats painted in bright colours can still be seen at

North Landing, Flamborough, where the precipitous angle of the shore has caused the evolution of a hull shape peculiar to this situation. Painted fishing boats are still a feature of many continental ports and harbours, particularly in the less frequented areas of the south. Trips in fishing boats however did nothing to change the existing scene other than by keeping a few more fishermen in business and enabling them to spend a little more on maintaining their craft.

The real impact of holiday boating came with the introduction of regular long distance services. The service from London to Margate via Gravesend was opened in 1815, nearly 30 years earlier than the first regular steamer service from Folkestone to Boulogne. Luxury steamers were introduced on the Margate run in the 1820s and it was not long before the whole of the south and east coasts, from the Norfolk resorts to Hampshire and Dorset, were accessible by scheduled boat services from London.

The paddle steamer was the vessel which dominated these routes and it remained in regular use until the outbreak of the Second World War (and in a few instances until after it). The earliest routes to close in the twentieth century were those which came into direct competition with fast train services from London. Those serving the Bristol Channel resorts, where a trip by pleasure boat from Ilfracombe to Tenby is a pleasant day's outing and an impossibility by rail, are still operating. Unfortunately we are unlikely ever again to see a paddle steamer disembarking holiday crowds at the head of an English pier. This was one of the most evocative sights of the twenties and thirties, and now one of the most nostalgic memories. The smell of the smoke and steam, the hoot of the whistle, the thunder of the paddle wheels, the crowds of men in striped blazers, white flannels and straw boaters, and the women in gay dresses and hats, the shouts of children and the general air of excitement add up to a microcosm of the English at the seaside in the troubled years between the wars. Now only the piers survive.

131

The *Essex Queen*. **One of the many paddle steamers plying between London and the south and east coast resorts during the first half of the century**

Port Soderic, Isle of Man. The cliff lift, transferred from the Falcon Cliff Hotel, Douglas, and closed in 1959

Sandgate Hill Railway, Folkestone, in 1911, seven years before closure

The seafront at Le Havre, devoid of motor cars but with an electric tram, in the years before the First World War

West Lift, Folkestone

WEYMOUTH. Showing King Georges statue.

DOUGLAS, HARRIS PROMENADE

DOUGLAS BAY HOTEL & MARINE DRIVE, I.O.M.

Dunluce Castle Co. Antrim.

Mumbles Pier, Swansea.

Top left
Folkestone West lift in 1912

Middle left
Harris Promenade, Douglas, Isle of Man

Bottom left
The coastal tramway overlooking Dunluce Castle, County Antrim

Top right
Weymouth in the early 1920s, with coaches lined up and drivers touting for custom

Middle right
Douglas Bay Hotel, Isle of Man, showing the coastal tramway

Bottom right
Swansea. The now defunct Mumbles Railway which ran along the shore from Swansea to Mumbles pier

Many piers originally bore railways that were built to serve the boats and convey passengers and their luggage to and from the pierhead. A few have survived and have since been transformed as pleasure lines. Those at Southend and Southport still have a functional justification because of the great lengths of the two piers, but the only justification for the railways at Felixstowe or Walton-on-the-Naze, along with many others, is simply the pleasure of the ride. It is unfortunate that a number of other seaside railways and tramways succumbed before the present interest in archaic transport became sufficiently strong to make obsolete lines economically viable (as at Ravenglass, Portmadoc, and across Romney Marsh to Dungeness). The miniature tramway along the edge of Brighton beach is still one of the best known features of that resort, but the more interesting Volk's Electric Railway, which ran from the Aquarium to Black Rock, was washed away and never replaced. The rails on which Volk's railway ran were below the water line, the passenger car being supported on a stiltlike framework. The wheels were driven by electric motors mounted on the platform and supplied with power from an overhead cable. A passenger platform on stilts known as Le Pont Roulant crossed the harbour at St Malo in the early years of the century.

The most interesting survival of a form of transport peculiar to the seaside is the collection of cliff lifts and inclined plane railways around the coasts of Britain. These ingenious and extremely economical devices are good examples of the way in which a form of transport can be intrinsically attractive. Some of them are also excellent pieces of Victorian engineering, demonstrating a nineteenth century genius for solving complex problems by employing the simplest of scientific principles. The north of England led the way, not unnaturally considering its terrain. A vertical lift was built at Saltburn in 1869; it was renewed in 1884 and is still in operation. The twin cabins are propelled by filling a tank beneath the upper car with water, thus

Goat cart, Weymouth, photographed in 1931

Below
Children's pony cart, c.1930

Weston-super-Mare showing, among other things, the invalid carriages which were a ubiquitous feature of the seaside at least until the outbreak of war in 1914

Below
Walton-on-the-Naze. Pier railway locomotive

forcing it to descend and haul up the lower car. At the bottom the tank is emptied and the cycle is repeated from the top. Scarborough followed closely after Saltburn, and the South Cliff, built in 1874-76, is now the oldest surviving cliff railway still in regular use. The Scarborough lifts have always been a popular way of making the passage over the precipitous cliffs from the town at the top to the spa, beach and harbour at the bottom. They also offer extremely attractive rides. A second lift was opened in 1880 and those at St Nicholas and the North Cliff in 1930 and 1931 respectively.

The longest and possibly most spectacular of English cliff railways runs between Lynton and Lynmouth in North Devon. The 900 foot plunge down a nearly 45 degree slope, in a car with an observation platform offering magnificent views of the tiny resort and the spectacular cliffs beyond, must be the best value for money obtainable on any transport system. The last lift to be built was the Fisherman's Walk lift at Bournemouth. With two others, at East Cliff and West Cliff (both built in 1908), it remains in use to this day. At the height of their popularity in 1904 the Metropole Hotel in Folkestone had its own private lift, but this was closed during the First World War and never re-opened. Another private lift was built for the Falcon Cliff Hotel, Douglas, in 1927.

Some of the seaside tramways, although not tackling the same gradients, offered similar experiences to the lifts. The coastal tramways of the Isle of Man passed through some very fine scenery as did others in Ireland. The Great Orme Railway at Llandudno which runs to the summit of the headland was opened in 1902 and continues to be one of the attractions of the town. The trams are hauled by cables laid beneath the centre of the tracks, the engine for which was changed from steam to electricity as late as 1958. The Great Orme Railway has demonstrated that it is possible for a tramway system which caters almost entirely for holidaymakers to continue to operate at a profit whilst retaining a slightly anachronistic charm.

It is easy to look back on such things as old railways or horse-drawn vehicles and to develop feelings towards them never experienced by their original passengers. New means of transport are nearly always welcomed by those who have to make regular use of them and sentiment has little place in an efficient transport system. Having said that, it has to be recognised that when catering for holiday traffic transport as such is less important than providing an enjoyable experience. For this reason archaic, uncomfortable or even normally uneconomic methods can be made attractive at the seaside. Had some of the older examples survived there is little doubt they would now be welcomed by crowds of enthusiasts.

One delightful aspect of seaside transport that has all but disappeared is the children's ride. Increasing amounts of motor traffic have made it unsafe to put most of these diminutive vehicles on present day roads and nothing replaces them. Old pictures show the charm of tiny dogcarts and goatcarts, miniature milk floats and the like, which were lined up for hire alongside the grown-ups' vehicles. Another feature now completely lost is the invalid carriage, a reminder of the time when the seaside was resorted to for health as much as for holidays, and when elderly invalids could outnumber holidaymakers in the off season at the fashionable resorts. In the first decades of this century the Bath chair cropped up in nearly every picture of a promenade. Lean men in bowler hats pushed rug-covered ladies and gentlemen in their three-wheeled basketwork or leather carriages along the seafronts to take the air, to enjoy the views, or to park in the shelters provided by the council, there to exchange reminiscences of service in outposts of Empire and of more prosperous youthful years.

Novelty has always exerted its maximum influence at the seaside in transport as in almost everything else. Even now open top buses are used in summer at many English resorts. Between

The Waterplane at Eastbourne

St. Leonards-on-Sea   The Marina.

Above
Novelty has always been an ingredient of seaside amusement, and postcard manufacturers have often responded to unusual events

Top left
Invalid carriages, Weymouth

Middle left
Bath chair, St Leonards, 1903

Bottom left
Le Pont Roulant, St Malo

Below
The railway station virtually on the beach at Ramsgate. Note the scenic railway on the pier in the background and the array of beach attractions in the foreground

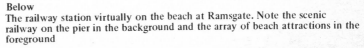

Côte d'Emeraude
1904. - SAINT-MALO. - Le Pont Roulant à marée haute - G. F.

the wars aircraft were exploited for the 'ten bob flips' that were likely to be the only experience of air travel ever to come within the means of most holidaymakers. In an age of jet travel the excitement of small craft is still strong, and Clacton airfield continues to offer the short 'joyride' flights that were pioneered there before the war.

Unfortunately the car has done little to improve the scene and much to spoil it, although some of the newer European and English motorways have demonstrated that this need not be so. No great enterprise is likely to appear able to spend sums equivalent to the present day value of the £50,000 which was the cost of Llandudno railway station in the last century. But new forms of transport are in themselves of great interest. One in particular, the hovercraft, has already made an impact on the Channel coasts of France and England. Another, the monorail, is offered as a fairground attraction; how likely it is to have some more practical application, such as conveying families from car parks to the beach, as the trams once did from the station, we shall have to wait and see.

POSTSCRIPT

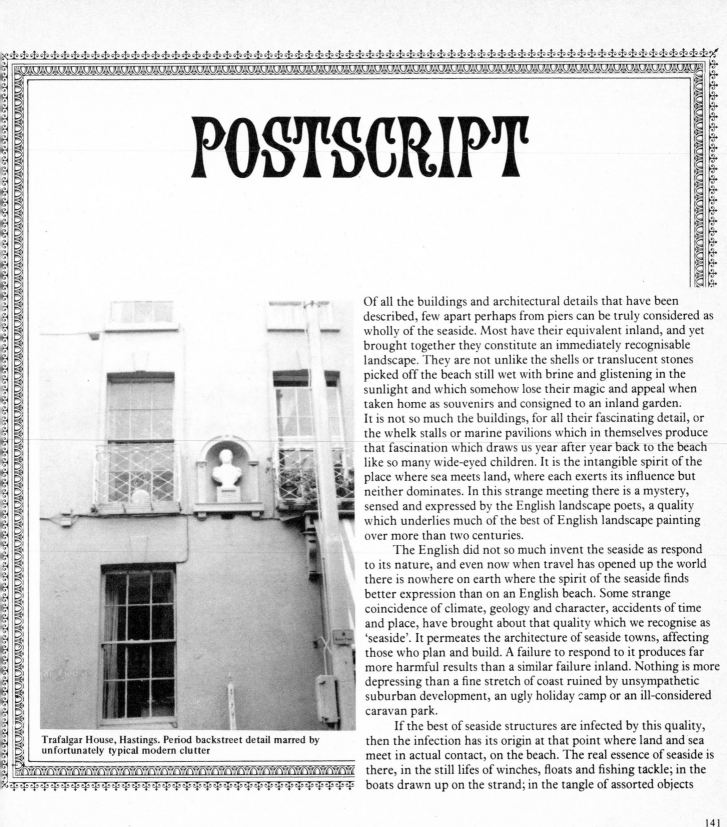

Trafalgar House, Hastings. Period backstreet detail marred by unfortunately typical modern clutter

Of all the buildings and architectural details that have been described, few apart perhaps from piers can be truly considered as wholly of the seaside. Most have their equivalent inland, and yet brought together they constitute an immediately recognisable landscape. They are not unlike the shells or translucent stones picked off the beach still wet with brine and glistening in the sunlight and which somehow lose their magic and appeal when taken home as souvenirs and consigned to an inland garden.

It is not so much the buildings, for all their fascinating detail, or the whelk stalls or marine pavilions which in themselves produce that fascination which draws us year after year back to the beach like so many wide-eyed children. It is the intangible spirit of the place where sea meets land, where each exerts its influence but neither dominates. In this strange meeting there is a mystery, sensed and expressed by the English landscape poets, a quality which underlies much of the best of English landscape painting over more than two centuries.

The English did not so much invent the seaside as respond to its nature, and even now when travel has opened up the world there is nowhere on earth where the spirit of the seaside finds better expression than on an English beach. Some strange coincidence of climate, geology and character, accidents of time and place, have brought about that quality which we recognise as 'seaside'. It permeates the architecture of seaside towns, affecting those who plan and build. A failure to respond to it produces far more harmful results than a similar failure inland. Nothing is more depressing than a fine stretch of coast ruined by unsympathetic suburban development, an ugly holiday camp or an ill-considered caravan park.

If the best of seaside structures are infected by this quality, then the infection has its origin at that point where land and sea meet in actual contact, on the beach. The real essence of seaside is there, in the still lifes of winches, floats and fishing tackle; in the boats drawn up on the strand; in the tangle of assorted objects

Teignmouth. Wheeled platforms used to give access to small boats in summer, stored in winter like strange insects on the car park

Branscombe. Beach monster

washed up on the tideline; in the driftwood carved by the sea and bleached by the sun; in the patterns left on the sands by the receding tide; and in the forms and textures of the rocks themselves. It is these which lure us to the sea's edge, and having done so exert on us that influence which produces seaside character and in its turn seaside architecture.

The seaside is one of the few remaining places where the child in every adult can find expression. It is where fathers build sand castles and mothers search rock pools for shells and sea anemones, as generations of English children and adults have done since the seaside was first discovered. If any attractions remain they are to be found among the simple and the timeless pleasures and the traditional attractions. Electronic and mechanical wonders come and go but Punch and Judy last for ever. When Punch dies the seaside will go with him. When we have lost sight of the simple pleasures, and above all when we have lost our sense of wonder, then we shall destroy the seaside as we have already destroyed so much of our inland environment. There is little sense of wonder to be found in a holiday camp or multi-storey hotel, little hope for simple pleasures when sun with sophistication is the dominant requirement.

There must always be on a tidal beach a strip of no man's land where each tide delivers or uncovers new treasures of flotsam and jetsam, of shell or stranded starfish. It is one of the advantages of the English coast and of the northern and western coasts of Europe that the rise and fall of the tides renews their beachscapes daily. The Mediterranean with no tide suffers in consequence. On the tidal beaches there is always something new to be found, and the change in the levels of the sea necessitates coastal works and strange gadgetry not encountered elsewhere. Over many centuries men have attempted to combat the sea and prevent it from eating away at the land or silting up harbours and driving ports inland. On the beaches exposed to the erosive effects of the sea (particularly along the North Sea coastline of

The wealth of rock forms, water, animal and plant life which provide constant change and interest on the shore

Below
Rocks, the fundamental architecture of the seaside

La Plage et les deux Jumeaux, Hendaye. A postcard view which conveys the atmosphere of the inter-war years as nostalgically and accurately as a jazz orchestra or 'flapper' dress

'Brighton Pierrots' by Walter Richard Sickert. Nothing could convey the atmosphere of the Edwardian seaside better than this painting of a concert party on the beach

Punch and Judy at Llandudno. The Punch and Judy show retains its popularity in spite of television and many prophesies of its demise. This one has particularly splendid decorations

Scarborough. A Piranesi-esque composition at beach level, supporting the promenade above

Below left
Rocks, water and shells, the essence of seaside

Below right
Sewage disposal on the Kent coast: an unfortunately common object

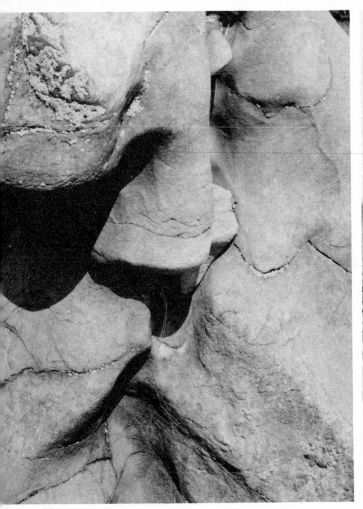

Left
Harwich. An amazing survival of a Georgian port. The street front makes no concessions to the proximity of the sea and could be paralleled in many inland towns in Essex. Other buildings in Harwich, which are more directly associated with the sea, have a distinctly nautical flavour. It was at a later date that holiday architecture began to appear, and Harwich owes the preservation of many interesting groups of buildings such as this to its failure as a holiday resort

Right
Scarborough

Below
Penzance. A superbly frivolous porch

Seaside vernacular at Portloe, Cornwall. Chapel and cottages built into the
hillside immediately above the inlet, displaying a response to the force of the
sea and the structure of the land

Budleigh Salterton. The naive sculpture of archaic equipment and fishing boats scattered about a pebbly shore, creating an intensely personalised place

Below
Hastings. A jellied eel stall which nicely paraphrases the vernacular style of the net lofts and avoids whimsy

Right
Broadstairs. Seaside notices

Below right
Dovercourt. The two lighthouses

Below
The weatherboarded and tarred wooden buildings in the old parts of some south and east coast towns (notably Hastings) are among the best known examples of vernacular seaside architecture. Many have been destroyed either for re-development or by wartime action, but their qualities have now been recognised and are sometimes reflected in the better recent buildings in these areas

Bournemouth. Sea defences: an entirely appropriate sculptural element
between sea and shore

Below
Budleigh Salterton

The Palace Pier, Brighton. A typical seaside view from the early years of this century. Perhaps the most notable change is in the number of people visible

Palace Pier, Brighton.

Below
Holland-on-Sea. Sea defences

Below
Hazards of the seaside, Lincolnshire

England) the remains and renewals of sea defence works make superb sculptural forms against sand, pebble and water and offer an unexplored archaeology. Where access to the sea has to be made without the aid of harbour or jetty strange machines lend character to the shore.

Less common now than they once were, monster platforms on cart or car wheels cluster like strange insects on the beach. Boats, hauled on to shingle ridges, engaging clutter of nets, floats, baskets, winches; these are the symbols of the seaside, the lasting images we perceive and recognise instantly as symbols of a place that has its being on two elements. Painted boats, their names and numbers in crude but vigorous lettering, all contribute to the scene. So do the encroachments which need to be guarded against. The sewage outfall, the decrepit caravan, the unsightly shack settlement, the bungalow estate, or the holiday camp that is no more than a collection of crudely designed and poorly sited hutments. The sea and the coastal landscape can absorb much, but there are physical and aesthetic limits to what can be tolerated.

Enough of the good remains as a living landscape to be recognised and enjoyed, but all the time it is being encroached upon. The ship chandler's shop and the seamen's mission, attractive leftovers from the past, are disappearing rapidly. And sadness lies not only in their destruction but in observing the quality of what replaces them. Yesterday's fascinating slot machines are now nearly all destroyed, or preserved in museums; their replacements are electronic gambling devices devoid of imagination or real originality. The word 'funfair' is now too often a misnomer for the tawdry places they have become. Transport has changed from a joy to a near nightmare, but the childlike delight in travel for its own sake remains to be revived by a re-incarnated steam railway, by a Great Orme Tramway or the latest cross-Channel hovercraft. Whether we acknowledge it or not the naïve and the childlike are components of our nature; they cannot be stifled, and nowhere are they better served than at the seaside. Where a need exists, means of satisfaction will be provided: with this in mind the future of the seaside and all that it stands for of fun, frivolity and outrageous fantasy can only be viewed with optimism.

APPENDIX I

A List of Pleasure Piers of England and Wales, with relevant Acts and other information.

This list, the only one known to exist, has been compiled from a variety of sources. The author has not been able to visit all the places mentioned and the details given are as accurate as possible in the circumstances. There is no clear distinction between a pleasure pier and a harbour pier, and those listed are considered to fall predominantly into the former category. Most were built primarily as promenade piers or as jetties for pleasure steamers. Considerable assistance has been given by the Ministry of Transport, and this is acknowledged with gratitude.

ABERYSTWYTH (non-statutory).

BANGOR (*Bangor Corporation Pier Act 1894*) length 1,550 feet with floating pontoon.

BLACKPOOL NORTH PIER (*Blackpool Pier Act & Orders 1863-1920*) length 2,130 feet including landing jetty.

BLACKPOOL SOUTH PIER (*Blackpool, South Pier, Orders, 1866-1920*) length 1,626 feet.

BLACKPOOL SOUTH SHORE (VICTORIA) PIER (*Blackpool, South Shore, Pier Orders, 1891 & 1924*).

BOGNOR (*Bognor Pier Order 1909*) length 1,000 feet: built in 1865, taken over by the Corporation in 1910 and later sold.

BOSCOMBE (*Boscombe Pier Order 1903*) length 600 feet.

BOURNEMOUTH (*Bournemouth Pier Act & Orders 1856-1903*) length 988 feet: original pier extended on rails and could be withdrawn in stormy weather.

BRIGHTON MARINE PALACE & PIER (*Brighton Marine Palace Pier Acts & Orders 1888-1952*) length 1,710 feet: deck area 126,000 sq ft: built to replace the Chain Pier (opened 1823, collapsed 1896): opened 1901.

BRIGHTON WEST PIER (*Brighton West Pier Acts & Orders 1866-1954*) length 1,150 feet.

BURNHAM (*Burnham, Somerset, Pier Order 1906 & Act 1907*) never completed.

CLACTON-ON-SEA (*Clacton-on-Sea Pier Acts & Orders 1866-1938*) built 1873: pavilion added in 1890s.

CLEETHORPES (*Cleethorpes Pier Order 1867 & Act 1873*) length 1,019 feet: opened 1870.

CLEVEDON *(Clevedon Pier Acts & Orders 1864-88)* length 850 feet: built 1869: constructed from factory-made components: has to accommodate a tidal rise and fall of 40 feet: purchased by the town in 1891 (now partially demolished).

COLWYN BAY *(Colwyn Bay, Victoria, Pier Order 1923)* length 1,365 feet.

CROMER *(Cromer UDC Act 1948)* length 500 feet: built in 1901 to replace a jetty destroyed by storm in 1897.

DEAL *(Deal Pier Order 1920)* concrete construction.

EASTBOURNE *(Eastbourne Pier Orders 1864-1900)*.

FELIXSTOWE *(Felixstowe Pier Order & Act 1900 & 1947)* length 3,960 feet: built 1904: pier railway.

FLEETWOOD *(Fleetwood Victoria Pier Order 1907)*.

GREAT YARMOUTH (BRITANNIA) *(Great Yarmouth New Britannia Pier Act & Order 1899 & 1952)* length 810 feet.

GREAT YARMOUTH (WELLINGTON) *(Great Yarmouth Wellington Pier Orders 1901 & 1921)*.

HASTINGS *(Hastings Pier Acts & Orders 1867-1937)*.

HERNE BAY *(Herne Bay Pier Order 1952)* length 0.75 mile: built in 1873 and subsequently extended: third longest: pier railway.

LLANDUDNO *(Llandudno Pier Orders 1866-1908)* length nearly 2,400 feet.

LOWESTOFT (CLAREMONT) PIER *(Lowestoft, South, Pier Orders 1900 & 1912)*.

LOWESTOFT (SOUTH) PIER *(Lowestoft South Pier Orders 1900 & 1912)* length 0.25 mile: harbour pier with amusement pavilion.

LYTHAM *(Lytham Pier Order 1864)*.

MARGATE *(Margate Pier Order 1878 & Harbour Act 1900)*.

MORECAMBE *(Morecambe Pier Orders 1896 & 1921)*.

MORECAMBE (WEST END) *(Morecambe, West End, Pier Orders 1893-1921)*.

MUMBLES *(Mumbles Railway & Pier Acts 1889-1939)*.

NEW BRIGHTON *(Wallasey Corporation Act 1927)*.

PAIGNTON *(Paignton Pier Act 1874)* length 800 feet.

PENARTH *(Penarth Promenade Pier Order 1924)* length 630 feet.

PORTSMOUTH *(Portsmouth Victoria Pier Order 1930)*.

REDCAR *(Redcar Pier Order 1949)* length 1,300 feet: opened 1873: repeatedly damaged by storm-driven ships.

RHYL *(Rhyl Pier Orders 1864 & 1912)* length nearly 0.50 mile.

RYDE *(Ryde Pier Order 1877)* consists of three piers, the Old Pier (pedestrian), the Tramway Pier and the Railway Pier.

SAINT ANNE'S-ON-SEA *(St Anne's-on-the-Sea Pier Orders 1879-1923)* opened 1885: enlarged and pavilion added 1904.

SALTBURN *(Saltburn & Marske-by-Sea UDC Act 1938)* damaged by ships and rebuilt.

SHANKLIN *(Shanklin Pier Order 1886)*.

SKEGNESS *(Skegness Pier Orders 1879 & 1946)*.

SOUTHEND *(Local Board Act 1887)* length 7,080 feet, the world's longest promenade pier: first section (1,500 feet) completed 1830: horse-drawn trams (now electric) along entire length: rammed six times by ships: present structure built 1889, extended 1897.

SOUTHPORT *(Southport Pier Order 1868)* built 1860 with a manually operated railway, replaced by a steam cable-railway in 1872: second longest.

SOUTHSEA *(Southsea South Parade Pier Order 1878)*.

SOUTHWOLD *(Southwold Pier Orders 1899 & 1949)*.

SWANAGE *(Swanage Pier Act & Orders 1859-1948)* length 1,400 fee steamer jetty adjoining an older structure originally used for loading Purbeck stone.

TEIGNMOUTH (non-statutory) length 600 feet.

TOTLAND BAY *(Totland Bay Pier Order 1879)*.

VENTNOR *(Ventnor Local Government Board Act 1884; Ventnor Pier Order 1910; Ventnor UDC Act 1931)* successor to two previous structures destroyed by storms.

WALTON-ON-THE-NAZE *(Walton-on-the-Naze Pier Orders 1864-9* extends 800 feet into 6 feet of water: pier railway.

WESTON-SUPER-MARE (BIRNBECK) *(Weston-super-Mare, Birnbeck, Pier Order 1896)* includes Birnbeck Island: length 1,100 feet: built 1867.

WESTON-SUPER-MARE (GRAND) *(Weston-super-Mare Grand Pi Acts 1893-1932)* built 1903-04.

WEYMOUTH *(Weymouth & Melcombe Regis Corporation Act 1887)* harbour pier with pavilion, etc.

WORTHING *(Worthing Pier Order 1920)* originally opened 1862: wrecked by storm 1913 and rebuilt.

YARMOUTH ISLE OF WIGHT *(Yarmouth IOW Pier and Harbour Order 1931)* length 700 feet: built 1876.

APPENDIX 2

A List of Cliff Railways.

Cliff railways although not entirely confined to the seaside are a part of the scene at many resorts and as such are one of the characteristic details of the English seaside. Like the piers many of them are Victorian in origin and the principles upon which they are worked form a fascinating study. The following details are extracted, with permission, from *Cliff Railways* by Geoffrey Body and Robert Eastleigh, published by David & Charles.

ABERYSTWYTH The only Welsh coastal cliff railway: opened 1896: 4 ft 10 in gauge: length 789 ft.

BOURNEMOUTH Three lifts: East Cliff lift opened 1908: length 170 ft: gradient 45 degrees. West Cliff lift opened 1908: length 145 ft: gradient 45 degrees. Fisherman's Walk lift built 1935 (the last to be built in England): length 128 ft: gauge in each case 5 ft 6 in.

BROADSTAIRS Opened 1910: near vertical 100 ft: gauge 5 ft 3 in.

DOUGLAS IOM Serves the Falcon Cliff Hotel: built 1927: gauge 5 ft: gradient 45 degrees: an earlier lift serving the hotel was sold and removed to Port Soderick.

FOLKESTONE Three built but one surviving: first cliff railway in south of England: opened 1885; gauge 5 ft 10 in: second double track added 1890; gauge 4 ft 10 in.

HASTINGS Two cliff railways: West Hill lift opened 1891: runs through tunnel: length 500 ft: gradient 1:3: gauge 6 ft. East Hill lift: opened 1903: gauge 5 ft: length 267 ft: gradient 1:1.28.

LYNTON & LYNMOUTH Longest in Britain: length 900 ft: gauge 3 ft 9 in: gradient 1:1.8: opened 1890.

MARGATE Cliftonville Lido lift: length 69 ft: gauge 5 ft: gradient 45 degrees.

SALTBURN Built 1884 to replace one built 1869: length 207 ft: gauge 4 ft 8½ in: gradient 1:1.33.

SCARBOROUGH Four lifts: South Cliff opened 1876 (the earliest surviving): length 284 ft: gauge 4 ft 8½ in: gradient 1:1.75. Central tramway opened 1880: length 234 ft: gradient 1:2: gauge 4 ft 8½ in. St Nicholas Cliff lift opened 1930: length 103 ft: gauge 7 ft 6 in: gradient 1:1.33. North Cliff lift opened 1931: length 166 ft: gauge 6 ft 6 in: gradient 1:2.

SOUTHEND Opened 1912: length 130 ft: gauge 4 ft 6 in: gradient 1:2.3.

TORQUAY Babbacombe Cliff railway opened 1926: length 716 ft: gauge 4 ft 8½ in: gradient 1:2.84.

WHITBY Cliff lift at West Cliff approached by a short tunnel into the cliff from the seawall.

157

INDEX

Sources of Illustrations
The author has contributed most of the photographs, prints and drawings reproduced in this book: other illustrations have been provided by, and are reproduced by kind permission of, the following:

Aerofilms Limited, pp 73 (bottom), 116/117
Mr F. C. Bolland, p 59
Club Mediterranée, p 115 (left)
Daily Telegraph, p 98
H. A. Hallas, p 75
Mr John Howarth, p 108 (top)
Leonore Mau, pp 96 (bottom), 97
Planair, p 109 (top)
Stichting Doelmatig Verzinken, pp 54/5